GET IELTS BAND 9
In Writing Task 2

OUR COMPLETE WRITING COURSE
WITH
75 BAND 9 MODEL ESSAYS

Containing Five Books of Expert Advice:

Book One: 15 Band 9 Model Essays

Book Two: IELTS Vocabulary Secrets

Book Three: 25 More Band 9 Model Essays

Book Four: IELTS Grammar Secrets

Book Five: Task 2 Essay Planning

This Paperback Edition Published by Cambridge IELTS Consultants
Cambridge, United Kingdom

PAGE INDEX

Introduction to Our Complete Course

The IELTS writing exam can be a very challenging test, even for native speakers of English. Part 2 of the writing test in particular (part 2 has the same format for both the Academic and the General Training types of IELTS) demands an extremely high standard if you are hoping to achieve a Band 7 or above.

Perhaps you have taken IELTS before and been disappointed with your writing result, or possibly you are planning to take it for the first time and are looking for guidance. Be assured that many thousands of people around the world have used our course to prepare for IELTS writing, and, as you can see from our five-star Amazon reviews, they have seen substantial improvements in what they achieve.

How have we achieved this? Over our many years of preparing students for IELTS and marking the exam itself, we have developed a series of methods which will help candidates gain the highest score they possibly can, even if their English is far from perfect. These methods involve analysing the possible types of Task 2 instructions you might get in the test, and preparing a structure to answer all of them. We also have rapid ways of developing your academic English to its maximum extent, by enhancing your advanced grammar skills and by building up your vocabulary in the specialised topics which always feature in the IELTS tests. By combining these methods together, we have seen many students increase their writing scores by two Band levels or more.

Whatever your reason for taking the test, we wish you the very best for it – and, of course, for all your future plans in life.

Jessica Alperne and Peter Swires
Course Editors, Cambridge IELTS Consultants

BOOK ONE

15 Band 9 Model Essays

Book One: 15 Band 9 Model Essays

Introduction to Book One

For many people, the most difficult part of the IELTS exam is often the Task 2 essay in the writing test. This is because not many candidates really understand the different types of Task 2 essay, or take the time to read examples of high quality essays before sitting the exam.

We are here to help.

In this book we show you how to analyze the Task 2 question, and we explain the different types of essays you may be asked to write. Most importantly, this book provides you with fifteen examples of Task 2 essays, all written to Band 9 standard. Each essay has accompanying comments from IELTS examiners which explain why the writing is Band 9 level, and a selection of advanced vocabulary which you can use in your own essays.

At the end of the book, there are a number of practice tasks for you to use. You should analyze the tasks and decide on which type they are. Then try to write your own essay in forty minutes, as you would in the exam. There is a key to the practice tasks, and also a summary of the ten most common mistakes in IELTS academic writing.

By following our advice and learning from these model essays, thousands of people around the world have seen huge increases in their IELTS writing band scores, allowing them to finally progress with their plans in life. We hope you will join them!

If you need a dictionary while reading, we recommend the free to use *Cambridge Dictionaries Online* from Cambridge University Press.

Jessica Alperne & Peter Swires
Cambridge IELTS Consultants
cambridgeielts@outlook.com

Explanation of the Different Types of Academic Task 2 Essay

There are two possible types of IELTS Academic Task 2 writing tasks: OPINION tasks and IDEAS tasks. Let's explain the difference, because this is very important.

Firstly, there are OPINION tasks, which ask for your opinion on a topic, such as whether you think something is a good or bad idea, or whether you support an idea. These OPINION tasks take two forms.

Some of these are OPINION > DISCUSSION tasks, which typically say *'Some people think that X is a good thing, while other people disagree. Discuss both sides and give your own view.'* Remember that the exact words used could be different (for example, it might say *'consider both aspects'* or similar) but the concept will be the same. In these OPINION > DISCUSSION tasks, you should write about each side of the discussion, and finally give your opinion at the end of your essay.

The other type of OPINION task is the OPINION > PERSONAL VIEWPOINT task. These tasks typically say *'X is a good thing. To what extent do you agree with this statement?'* Again, the exact words will often vary (for example, it might say *'Many people support the suggestion of X. How far do you support this proposal?'*) but the concept will be the same. In these OPINION > PERSONAL VIEWPOINT tasks, you should state your personal viewpoint at the *beginning* of the essay, and then explain why you have this opinion.

The second type of task are IDEAS tasks, which ask you to think of some ideas on a topic (such as the reasons for a problem or some ways to solve it) or to evaluate a situation. In these IDEAS tasks, you will get high marks for thinking of a number of ideas on the topic, but you will lose marks if you give a strong personal opinion.

The common IDEAS tasks are IDEAS > PROBLEM/SOLUTION, IDEAS > CAUSE/EFFECT and IDEAS > EVALUATE. This book has examples and explanations of all these types.

In the exam, you should analyze the task carefully *before* you start writing, to make sure you understand which type you need to write. Ask yourself: is this an OPINION or an IDEAS task? Is it asking me to give my personal view, or is it asking me to think of some ideas on a topic? Which type of OPINION or IDEAS task is it? Then you should spend a few minutes planning your essay with some simple notes. The final section in this book (Book Five: Essay Planning) has a full explanation of how to plan quickly and effectively using notes.

Don't try to write anything very different in structure from the models in this book. These model essays are exactly what the examiners want to see from you. Read our model essays, and then use our practice tasks to practice writing your own essays in a similar way.

Opinion Type Tasks: Model Essays

Example Task 1

You should spend about 40 minutes on this question.

Some people believe that sport is an essential part of school life for children, while others feel it should be purely optional. Discuss these opposing views and give your own opinion.

You should give reasons for your answer, and include ideas and examples from your own knowledge and experience.

Write at least 250 words.

Explanation of the task

This is an OPINION > DISCUSSION type task. It asks you to consider both sides of an argument, and then give your opinion. The classic plan for this type of essay is:

Introduction paragraph giving background but not your opinion

Main paragraph supporting side A of the discussion

Main paragraph supporting side B of the discussion

Conclusion paragraph summarizing and giving your opinion which supports side B

This layout ensures that there is a link between the second main paragraph and the conclusion which presents your opinion.

Model Essay 1

Sport continues to be a controversial topic in the school curriculum, just as sport itself has become a controversial industry in some respects. There are valid opinions on both sides, which I will consider now.

On the one hand, some people feel that sport uses up time which could be better spent on academic subjects such as exam preparation. In addition, it might be said that it is unwise to force children to do activities which they have no interest in. After all, some youngsters are just not sporty, and should be allowed to study instead. Finally, there are question marks over the wholesomeness of sport itself, with drugging and corruption scandals increasingly common, as we see in cycling at present. Some people believe that this lack of morals sets a poor example to young people.

On the other hand, though, one major benefit of sport is that it helps children's physical development at an important stage. If all their time was spent studying, they would become unfit and their minds would eventually suffer. Furthermore, supporters of school sport emphasize the importance of team building in sports such as football or hockey, which is often felt to be an excellent preparation for adulthood. Finally, many people feel that a competitive spirit, so important today, is fostered by sports at an early age. It is notable, for example, that many successful business people excelled in sport at school.

Overall, I feel that sport should be compulsory for school children, because the positive effect on their mental and physical development outweighs the negatives. This is as long as children are given a wide range to choose from, to ensure their interest is high, and that the sports industry itself maintains the highest standards of conduct.

(293 words)

Examiner's comments

This essay would receive Band 9. It exceeds the minimum word requirement and is clearly organized into introduction, main body discussion, and conclusion with opinion. The candidate has introduced the topic, and then given several relevant points on each side of the discussion. There are suitable examples at times, without too much detail. The conclusion has a clear and relevant opinion. The English used is clear and uncomplicated, with good use of common academic words, (e.g. *controversial, emphasize, excel.*) The ideas and paragraphs are connected by good use of common linking phrases (e.g. *on the one hand, furthermore, overall.)*

Example Task 2

Some people feel that it is always wrong to keep animals in captivity, for instance in zoos. Other people say that there are benefits for the animals and for humans. Discuss both sides of this debate, and give your personal view.

Explanation of the task

This is another OPINION > DISCUSSION type task. Although the topic and the words used in the instructions are different to the previous task, you should follow the same basic structure. You should discuss both sides objectively, describing two or three points on each side, and then give your view in the conclusion.

Model Essay 2

Zoos continue to be controversial, even now that they have evolved into 'animal parks' or similar facilities. Most people love animals, and there are strong views on both sides, which I will discuss now.

People opposed to zoos highlight the unnatural way in which animals live in such places. For example, captive animals do not need to hunt or raise offspring, and this means that they are not living as nature intended. Furthermore, the anti-zoo lobby point out that animals probably suffer mentally when kept in captivity, even if their surroundings are spacious and similar to the natural habitat. Symptoms of mental issues range from repetitive behaviour to eating disorders, and these are often seen in captive animals. Lastly, it is often said that zoos add little to animal conservation, which is better served by preserving their habitat.

Conversely, those who support zoos say that in most cases they offer a secure and peaceful setting for animals, for example in high quality wildlife parks or reserves. They add that in many cases, the animals would suffer from loss of habitat or poaching in the wild, and in captivity they are at least safe and able to breed successfully. Finally, zoo enthusiasts feel that zoos and animal parks are part of an integrated system of protecting animals, involving habitat protection, breeding programmes and disease control. This all helps to safeguard endangered species and thus preserve the global ecosystem for the future benefit of all life forms.

Overall, I feel that zoos provide a valuable service to society and the animal world, as they help to protect many species. This outweighs their possible disadvantages, as long as they are properly staffed and maintained.

(281 words)

Examiner's comments

This would be a band 9 essay. The style is academic but not excessively formal, and the writer gives a personal opinion without emotion or humour. Both sides of the topic are discussed, using clear examples to illustrate the points. There is a logical flow from the points supporting zoos into the conclusion, which also supports the zoos. The language used is academic (e.g. *conversely, thus*) without being technical or archaic. Linking phrases are used to guide the reader helpfully (e.g. *furthermore, overall.*) The conclusion includes a proviso (*as long as they are . . .*) which is a strong feature in academic writing.

Example Task 3

Some people believe that a gap year between school and university is a good idea, while others disagree strongly. Consider both sides of this debate and present your own opinion.

Explanation of the task

This is another OPINION > DISCUSSION type task. You should follow the same basic structure as for examples 1 and 2.

Model Essay 3

While gap years are increasingly popular, they continue to be rather controversial because the benefits are hard to quantify exactly. There are arguments on both sides of this very topical debate, and I will discuss them now.

On the one hand, opponents of gap years point to the cost involved in areas such as air fares, accommodation and living expenses. All this money has to come from the student's family, or even from borrowing to be paid later. Secondly, it is often said that gap years take a young person's focus away from studying, and allows them to get involved in distractions such as travelling. This can make it hard to adjust to university life, damaging the student's performance. Finally, there is a concern over the safety of young people if they are travelling to remote places. Being kidnapped or mugged is a poor start to an academic career, after all.

On the other hand, supporters of gap years say that the skills learned outweigh the disadvantages. They highlight the independence and assertiveness that a student will acquire, in areas such as time management and interpersonal skills. They also say that these skills lead to greater career success later in life, thus cancelling out the costs involved. Furthermore, there are many examples of young people using gap years to achieve something significant, whether in voluntary work or in a sector of business that interests them.

In conclusion, my own feeling is that a year off can indeed be a useful activity, with the experience leading to improved skills that are invaluable in the future. Of course, this is provided that the year is planned carefully and used for something genuinely worthwhile.

(281 words)

Examiner's comments

This is a good example of a Band 9 essay. The writer discusses each side of the debate, giving two or three points to support each side. The points are relevant and clear, without being too specific or personal. The linking words used (*e.g. On the other hand, furthermore, in conclusion*) show the reader how the essay develops and what to expect at each stage. The language is academic but understandable to a general reader. The opinion in the conclusion is expressed without emotion or attempts at humour.

Example Task 4

Some people think that it is best to save money, for example in a bank or savings scheme. Other people feel that money should be spent whenever it is available. Discuss these views and reach an opinion on this debate.

Explanation of the task

This is our final example of an OPINION>DISCUSSION type task.

Model Essay 4

The question of whether to save or spend money is very topical today, as so many people are struggling with financial worries. There are valid arguments on both sides, which I will discuss now.

On the one hand, it is often said that spending money is one way to relax and enjoy life, for instance by shopping or taking holidays, and there is certainly some truth in this. In addition, we usually have no choice but to spend quite a large proportion of our available salary on day to day expenses such as food, housing and transport, and so there is surprisingly little remaining to save anyway. Finally, spending money on products and services boosts the economy and creates employment, and in this sense is a worthwhile action.

On the other hand, other people point out the dangers of reckless spending, for example on frivolous or unnecessary items, which is often encouraged by advertising. Young people in particular are vulnerable to being influenced like this. Furthermore, advocates of saving often point out that, without a reserve of funds for emergencies, unemployment or illness, people are putting themselves at risk of hardship or even bankruptcy. This is especially true in the current economic situation. Lastly on this side of the debate, people emphasise the need to accumulate wealth during one's lifetime, so that one's children can inherit money or property which will increase their security and standard of living.

Overall, I tend to agree that it is wiser to save money wherever possible, for reasons which benefit both individuals today and future generations.

(263 words.)

Examiner's comments

This is a Band 9 essay. As the examiner, it is immediately clear to me in the first paragraph that the writer is introducing an OPINION > DISCUSSION essay, which the task requires. The two sides of the topic are then discussed in logical paragraphs, with a series of simple examples to support each side. The linking phrases help to introduce each example (E.g. *On the one hand, in addition, finally,)* and they also show me the stages of the essay (E.g *Overall* to introduce the conclusion.) The English used is reasonably academic (E.g. *Large proportion, emphasize the need)* and the sentences are generally clear. The reader gets the impression that the writer is rational and well-informed, and able to discuss a topic objectively.

Example Task 5

It is better to save money than to spend it.

How far do you agree with this statement? Is saving more important than spending in today's world?

Explanation of the task

This is an OPINION > PERSONAL VIEWPOINT type task. It asks you to say how much you agree with an idea. You should state your opinion at the start, and then explain why you have this opinion, giving several logical reasons. You should briefly mention the opposing view as well. The conclusion should be a summary of your viewpoint.

Note that this type of essay is different from the OPINION > DISCUSSION type.

Model Essay 5

With the world in such economic turmoil, many of us face difficult choices in managing our money. Personally, I feel that saving is preferable to high spending, and I will explain why.

Firstly, saving money is a sensible precaution in a world where the future is uncertain. It is possible, for example, that a person might meet unemployment, ill health or other crises at some point in life. It is essential to have some funds in reserve for these situations, and saving is for most people the only way to achieve this. Furthermore, I believe that saving is itself a good discipline for people to develop, as it builds skills of planning and reaching targets. We can see this in the way that disciplined people build up quite large sums through small monthly contributions to savings plans. In many cases this meets important objectives in their lives, including large purchases such as cars or property. Finally, we have to remember the reasons for the current economic problems besetting the world. The crisis was caused by excessive spending and insufficient saving – not just by individuals, but by corporations and even governments themselves. I feel that an emphasis on sensible saving should be a universal strategy now.

I do appreciate that some people think differently, saying that it is better to live for the moment and spend accordingly. While some daily spending is essential, of course, I feel this is a potentially unwise viewpoint, especially considering recent global events.

To conclude, I believe that saving is the wiser course, not just for financial but also for personal and political reasons. Sensible saving is an invaluable skill and a buffer against uncertainty.

(279 words)

Examiner's comments

This would be a Band 9 essay. It exceeds the minimum word count and is organized in clear paragraphs. The writer introduces the topic briefly, and then states his/her viewpoint in the introduction. There are then three clear and logical reasons to justify the viewpoint, with some simple examples that can be understood by anyone with a general awareness of the world. The opposing view is mentioned briefly, and then rejected, so the essay is not completely one-sided. The conclusion re-states the writer's opinion and summarizes without repeating details. The English is formal/academic, but not complicated. The choice of words is academic (e.g. *turmoil, insufficient, invaluable*) but still clear. There are clear linking phrases to guide the reader through the stages of the essay (e.g. *firstly, finally, to conclude.*)

Example Task 6

'Tourism is always a force for good which enables people of different countries to understand each other.'

To what extent do you agree with this idea?

Explanation of the task

This is another OPINION > PERSONAL VIEWPOINT type task. *'To what extent do you agree . . .?'* is the key phrase that tells you this. You should start by saying how much you agree with the statement, and then explain why you think this. You should briefly consider the opposing view, even though you then reject it.

Model Essay 6

The role of tourism in the world today is widely debated, with some people claiming that it is indeed a force for international understanding. However, I personally do not entirely accept this, and I will explain why in this essay.

Firstly, we must consider the potential negatives of contact between cultures. For example, when western tourists visit untouched parts of the world, their stay causes pollution for local societies. We see this in the litter left at Machu Picchu in Peru, and in the damage to ecology caused by safari tourism in Africa. Furthermore, there are numerous examples of tension between tourists and local cultures, ranging from drunken British tourists in Europe to American 'spring breakers' in Canadian or Latin American resorts. In these cases, tourism actually leads to resentment and distrust between nationalities, not better understanding.

A further reason to be wary of this idea is the economic aspect. It is sometimes said that tourism improves international relations because it encourages the flow of money from wealthy to less developed countries. In reality, however, the wealth generated usually stays in the hands of private companies or local officials, and rarely drips down into the population. Many of us have visited less developed nations as tourists, and have witnessed at first hand the poverty that exists outside the confines of the resort hotels. We leave with the impression that our stay has contributed nothing to the lives of those we have observed.

This is not to say that tourism is entirely bad, of course. There are benefits in terms of improving local infrastructure such as roads and airports. But to say that it is 'always a force for good' is to ignore the various problems it causes.

(289 words)

Examiner's comments

I would certainly give this essay a band 9 score. The writer answers the task completely, and makes his/her opinion clear in the introduction. The main body contains a series of clear reasons to justify this opinion, using examples which are relevant and accessible to the general reader. The writer mentions the opposing view briefly *('There are benefits in terms of improving local infrastructure such as roads and airports'*) so that the essay has some balance.

Example Task 7

'We should introduce laws to make businesses and state services employ equal numbers of male and female workers in every department or area of the company.'

How far would you support this proposal?

Explanation of the task

This is another OPINION > PERSONAL VIEWPOINT type task. The instruction *'How far do you support this idea'* tells you this.

Model Essay 7

The issue of equality for men and women at work is still widely debated, despite the extensive legislation that now exists in many countries. Personally, I do not feel that imposing a numerical target for gender is a sensible idea, and I will explain why.

Firstly, we have to consider whether equal numbers of men and women really wish to do every job which is available. For example, few women wish to be airline pilots, and only a minority of school teachers are male. If we impose a law on airlines or schools, where will they find the people to fill these posts willingly? Furthermore, there is the huge issue of the existing workforce. Would it be right to dismiss a worker because he or she is of a certain gender, in order to create a statistically perfect balance? The effects would be disastrous for many hard-working people. Finally, I believe we should find ways to encourage equality of opportunity through support and guidance, rather than top-down legislation. For instance, improved child care facilities and subsidies would probably encourage more women into parts of the workforce which may currently be difficult to enter.

I do understand the opposing view, which is that legislation is the quickest and most effective way to achieve gender equality. Nevertheless, I feel that the disruptive effects of 'overnight' legislation would destabilise society and hinder many people's prospects.

Overall, I believe that equality is an excellent goal for society to strive for. Above all, though, I think that this needs to be a gradual process, based on careful support rather than sudden legislation.

(267 words)

Examiner's comments

This essay would achieve Band 9. It is presented in a clear form, with obvious paragraphs to separate the introduction, main body, concession and conclusion. The writer shows that this is an OPINION > PERSONAL VIEWPOINT essay by introducing the topic and then giving his opinion in the first paragraph. The writer explains the opinion by giving three clear reasons, each one supported by an example which is readily understandable to a general reader.

Example Task 8

"Prison is the only truly effective form of punishment, because it separates criminals from society."
To what extent do you support this view?

Explanation of the task

This is another OPINION > PERSONAL VIEWPOINT essay. The task may be phrased as *'How far do you support x/ To what extent do you support x/ In what ways do you agree with x'* or any similar wording. Be alert to the different possible ways that this can be expressed, and remember the difference between this type and the OPINION > DISCUSSION type task.

Model Essay 8

There is no doubt that we need to find effective forms of punishment for criminals, and also find ways to protect citizens from the threat of crime. I personally feel that prison is only one of a range of options we should use, and is not always the most effective.

Firstly, I do not accept that all criminals need to be separated from society. Juvenile and minor offenders can be punished through fines, community service or other non-custodial means. This is cheaper than prison, and prevents the damage to the criminal's family which in itself could generate further social problems. Furthermore, by keeping these small-scale criminals in society, we can try to rehabilitate them, for example through training or education programmes. This will help to reduce re-offending in future.

Besides this, if offenders are believed to be a threat to their fellow citizens, there are ways of containing them such as electronic tagging, curfews or regular reporting to the police. Such methods have been shown to be effective in reducing criminal behaviour and are themselves quite a strong punishment, as they restrict an offender's freedom greatly. Finally, we should remember that prisons are to some extent 'schools of crime' and in many cases prisoners end their jail terms as more capable and determined criminals than when they entered.

Of course, it is true that in certain cases we need to both punish criminals and isolate them from other people. I recognise that violent or dangerous people need to be imprisoned – yet I believe this applies to a small minority of instances.

To conclude, I feel that prison is a last resort in cases where there is no alternative. This does not make it the only effective punishment, but rather the most severe among a variety of possibilities.

(290 words)

Examiner's comments

This meets the standard for a band 9 essay. The writer introduces the topic and then makes his/her opinion clear. The main body then contains a small range of reasons explaining this opinion, signposted with linking words (*e.g. Firstly, furthermore besides this, finally*) which guide the reader through the stages. The English used in the essay is academic but clear and modern. The writer shows that he has considered the opposing view briefly *('I recognise that violent or dangerous people need to be imprisoned . . .')* so that the essay has some balance. The reader feels that the writer is a logical thinker, able to organise ideas in support of his opinion.

Ideas Type Tasks: Model Essays

Example Task 9

Many people today are worried about 'cybercrime' such as hacking and identity theft. What problems does 'cybercrime' cause, and what solutions can you suggest for ordinary people and businesses to take?

Explanation of the task

This is an IDEAS > PROBLEM/SOLUTION type essay. It does *not* ask for your opinion about a topic, such as whether you think cybercrime is important or not. It asks you to think of some *problems* in a situation, and suggest some *solutions* to these problems. In tasks such as this, you should introduce the topic, describe two or three problems, then offer two or three solutions, and then summarize in the final paragraph.

Remember, this is *not* an OPINION type task. You will lose marks if you give a strong personal opinion in this essay.

Model Essay 9

Cybercrime is a cause of widespread concern today, as so many people use technology to store and transmit sensitive data. There are a number of problems that people suffer as a result of these crimes, but also some straightforward measures we can take to protect ourselves.

Perhaps the worst problem stemming from this is the financial impact. If someone has his or her bank account emptied, or has false credit lines created under their name, they are potentially liable for large sums of money. Even if they can avoid the consequences, their bank or finance company has to cover the losses, which can damage their performance. A further problem is the way in which these stolen funds are used to subsidize other crimes, such as drug distribution or even terrorism. Once the money enters the criminal networks, we have no way of knowing how it will be used. Finally, there is the problem of anxiety and stress caused to the innocent victims of these crimes. The initial shock is often followed by months or years or legal wrangling, paperwork and a sense of insecurity.

Turning to possible solutions, probably the most effective measure is to improve personal security, ranging from passwords to the shredding of documents. This denies the criminals the raw materials to work with. Secondly, we should raise awareness of the risks among the elderly or the very young – two groups who are often specifically targeted – via publicity and public education. Ultimately, however, it is the financial companies who can make the greatest contribution, by increasing their security and detection systems – ideally in partnership with the police.

Overall, the problems caused are both financial and social, and the solutions should involve coordinated action by individuals, corporations and the state.

(288 words)

Examiner's comments

This would receive a Band 9 score. The essay is clearly organized into sections, within which there are linking words (e.g. *a further problem, Turning to, ultimately, overall*) which signpost the ideas. The writer describes three problems and then three solutions, using relevant examples that do not rely on technical knowledge. The examples are presented in a variety of ways (e.g. *such as, ranging from/to.*)The English is fairly formal (e.g. *potentially liable, consequences, initial shock*) but always modern and clear. The essay describes a controversial subject without any bias or emotion, and no personal opinion is given.

Example Task 10

Many people today are worried about young children using video games. What problems might these games cause, for children and society as a whole? How could these problems be reduced?

Explanation of the task

This is an IDEAS > PROBLEM/SOLUTION essay. It uses the word 'problems' clearly, and then asks for solutions in a paraphrased way (*'How could these problems be reduced?')*

Remember that the exact words *'problem'* and *'solution'* may not be used in the task; you must be alert to synonyms such as *'challenge'* and *'answer.'*

Model Essay 10

The almost universal availability of video games among children has presented us with a number of challenges and decisions, none of which are straightforward. I believe there are three main problems associated with these products, and also three remedies we can adopt.

Perhaps the major problem we need to deal with is the level of violence found in these games. Many of them feature aggressive or warlike characters, ranging from soldiers to criminals and killers. This inevitably leads children to believe that such behaviour is normal, or even desirable. A second issue is the obsessive way that some children use the games – for example, preferring their computers to real friendships, making these children isolated and socially naïve. Finally, there are physical effects from excessive gaming, including eye strain, insomnia and damage to posture. These can be difficult to reverse once they have taken hold.

Turning to possible solutions, one key step would be to legislate more strictly to control the content of these games. They could, for instance, be reviewed by censors in the same way that films are. This would prevent unsuitable material influencing young minds. To tackle the problem of obsessive use, we could make more counselling and advice available through schools. On the subject of physical side effects, advice on safe use could be included as part of the packaging or even the game itself, so that youngsters are constantly aware of the risks.

To sum up, this is a problem that has both social and physical effects, and the solution will require combined action by manufacturers, schools and authorities.

(261 words)

Examiner's comments

This essay would be marked at Band 9. The writer introduces the topic well, and makes it clear in the first paragraph that this will be an IDEAS > PROBLEM/SOLUTION essay. The ideas described are relevant and clear, without too much detail or technical description. The English used features some strong academic vocabulary (E.g. *desirable, obsessive, unsuitable)* and is clear to the general reader. The writer uses conditionals effectively (*could, would*) to propose ideas, showing that he has considered the outcomes of his suggestions.

Example Task 11

In many countries today, there are concerns about the unhealthy lifestyles that people lead. What health issues are linked to modern lifestyles? What answers to these problems can you suggest?

Explanation of the task

This is another IDEAS > PROBLEM/SOLUTION type task. *'Issues'* and *'answers'* are common synonyms for *'problems'* and *'solutions.'* You should think of two or three problems, and then a similar number of solutions. Remember, you do not need to have any specialist knowledge to discuss this topic. *'Your own experience'* means things you have read or seen in the media, whether in your own country or around the world.

Model Essay 11

Most people agree that modern lifestyles can be unhealthy, both physically and mentally. I believe there are three main problems, but also some practical steps we can take.

Perhaps the largest problem is the issue of obesity, which is growing drastically in most Western countries. With people working at desks and using transport rather than walking, weight gain seems inevitable, and being overweight causes various medical issues including heart trouble and strokes. Another major problem linked to lifestyle is poor diet, with people who are short of time eating junk food rather than proper nutrients. Resultant health problems range from obesity to high cholesterol and even organ failure. Finally, we must consider the issue of mental health. Modern lifestyles are highly pressurised, with people expected to work at a fast pace for extended periods, and little scope for family life or relaxation, leading to enormous stress and anxiety.

Turning to possible solutions, the biggest step would be to improve the level of education regarding health issues connected to lifestyle, especially obesity. The government, media and schools should work together to raise awareness of the dangers and to promote sports and other positive practices. A further step would be to use legislation to curb the consumption of unhealthy foods, for example by imposing higher sales taxes or by restricting availability in retail outlets. Furthermore, to deal with the psychological impacts, we should encourage employers to adopt more flexible working practices, allowing workers to lead a fuller private life with less stress.

Overall, the key problems of obesity and stress can be addressed through a combination of awareness, targeted legislation and better employment practices.

9271 words)

Examiner's comments

This essay deserves a Band 9 score. The writer gives a brief introduction to the topic, and then gives three relevant examples of the problems, using generally available evidence. Each idea is introduced with a helpful linking phrase (*E.g. 'Turning to, furthermore.')* The writer suggests three sensible solutions, and considers their impact on the situation. The summary is brief but comprehensive, and paraphrases the main ideas well. The vocabulary used throughout the essay is modern and formal/academic in tone (*E.g. 'scope, inevitable, legislation.')*

Example Task 12

Having police officers patrolling the streets is often considered an essential way to reduce crime. How effective do you think police street patrols are? What other ways of reducing crime can you propose?

Explanation of the task

This is an IDEAS > EVALUATE type essay. It does not ask you to give an opinion about the principle of police patrols, but to consider how effective they are, and to suggest other ways to reduce crime. You should introduce the topic, then describe how effective you think patrols are, then propose two or three alternatives, then summarize.

Model Essay 12

We are all keen to reduce crime wherever possible, and the role of visible policing is a hotly debated part of this. Personally, I feel that street patrols are highly effective, although there are several supplementary methods too.

Regarding the effectiveness of patrols, evidence suggests that an increase in police on the streets leads directly to a drop in crime, especially crimes of violence and robbery. This was the experience of New York when it adopted the 'zero tolerance' policy in the 1990s, a high-profile policing tactic which has been extended successfully to many other cities worldwide. When compared to other tactics that have been tried, ranging from citizen patrols to CCTV, there is little doubt that assertive police patrolling is the most effective resource we have.

Turning to other methods, we should supplement police patrols with coordinated action elsewhere in the state. For instance, the courts should be prepared to issue deterrent sentences and prisons should be run strictly. This would help to deter people from committing crimes in the first place. Secondly, we should increase the resources available to the police away from the streets as well, for instance in detective and forensic departments, hopefully ensuring that detection rates are high when crimes do occur. Moreover, individuals and businesses should step up their own security arrangements to complement the police presence. For example, improved locks and lighting are simple measures which can reduce theft and burglary.

All in all, I feel that visible police patrols have been proved to be the most effective way to reduce common crimes. Their effectiveness can be maximized by supporting action from elsewhere in the police and justice system, and by private citizens doing their part as well.

(285 words)

Examiner's comments

This would be a Band 9 essay. The writer introduces the topic in an impersonal way, then gives his evaluation with reference to credible evidence and examples which support his assessment. The writer then describes several other measures and summarizes briefly. The English is academic and fairly formal, but the sentences are clear and the vocabulary is not over specialized. There are clear paragraphs for each section, and good use of linking words to move between points.

Example Task 13

Many countries today are experiencing high levels of migration from rural areas to cities. What are the causes of this trend, and what effects does it have on the existing city dwellers?

Explanation of the task:

This is an IDEAS > CAUSE/EFFECT type essay. It asks you to think of some causes of the situation, and also some effects. It does not ask for your opinion about whether something is good or bad. You should introduce the topic, then describe two or three causes, then two or three effects. There should be a short summary at the end.

Model Essay 13

Migration from the countryside to cities is certainly a topical issue, as so many nations are seeing this pattern today. There are three main causes, and two key impacts, which I will outline now.

The main cause is probably the lack of employment available to rural people. Rural industries, ranging from agriculture to food production and animal breeding, have all been rationalized and made far more efficient in recent years, meaning that fewer people are needed to staff them. Furthermore, the growth of employment opportunities in the cities means that people, especially youngsters, are tempted to move there by higher wages and the prospect of reliable work. Finally, many countries still have a weaker infrastructure in rural areas, especially in terms of transport and economic activity. For example, if a country dweller is unable to find public transport to get to work locally, that person will inevitably consider moving to a city where the infrastructure is far better established.

Regarding the effects felt by the urban residents, perhaps the main impact is on accommodation. An increased urban population drives up the cost of buying or renting a home, leading to possible hardship for people who had assumed that prices would remain stable. We can see this clearly in major conurbations such as London, Sao Paolo or Delhi, where property prices are extremely high and continue to rise. The other main effect on the existing city population is the vastly increased competition for job opportunities, especially at a less skilled level. For instance, drivers, shop workers and hospitality staff find themselves competing for work with new arrivals who are often prepared to work for less. This can lead to a reduction in wages and consequent decline in standard of living, especially when combined with the increased cost of housing.

To sum up, the causes of this trend are primarily to do with employment, and the effects are felt in terms of wages and accommodation.

(312 words)

Examiner's comments

This is a Band 9 essay. The writer introduces the topic, and describes three causes using clear, academic language (e.g. *rationalized, employment opportunities, infrastructure.)* The examples given are clear and relevant, and do not rely on specialized knowledge. The writer uses a variety of structures and marks each point with linking words (e.g. *furthermore, finally, regarding, to sum up*.) The word count is the maximum that an examiner would be prepared to read.

Example Task 14

In many countries, financial crime involving identity theft is increasing. What are the causes of this trend, and what effect does identity theft have on the victims involved?

Explanation of the task

This is another IDEAS > CAUSE/EFFECT type essay. You should try to use examples and evidence that you know about from the media, press or Internet, but do not give personal stories about yourself or people you know.

Model Essay 14

There is no doubt that identity fraud is a great concern, especially in western countries where people are most at risk. I think there are two main causes, and a number of damaging effects.

The major cause is probably the almost universal use of digital technology to store financial data and undertake financial transactions. It is surprisingly easy for criminals to obtain personal information about a possible victim, and then to use this information to impersonate the target. Because bank accounts and loans can be applied for digitally, without the need for face-to-face contact, the criminals are able to apply for financial products remotely, often before the victim is even aware of the attack. The second key cause is, I believe, the increasing probability of 'traditional' crimes (such as armed robbery, mugging or burglary) being detected. When criminals see the widespread use of CCTV, DNA profiling and fingerprinting, they are less inclined to indulge in such old-fashioned crimes. Rather, they prefer the lower risk and more profitable use of data-based crimes.

The effects on the unfortunate victims can be quite devastating. Firstly, there is the loss of money from bank accounts or by being connected to a fraudulent loan. In some cases, this can take years for the victim to pay back or resolve with the banks and the authorities. Secondly, there is the damage to their credit rating, which means they may find it impossible to obtain legitimate credit in future. In extreme cases, people's employment prospects can even be damaged as well, as they find themselves profiled as a financial risk.

Overall, the presence of technology and the decline of 'traditional' crimes are the key causes behind this trend. The effects on the victims involve long-term financial hardship in many instances.

(293 words)

Examiner's comments

We would give this essay a Band 9 grade. The writer provides three causes of the situation and describes three effects, which is a suitable number of ideas in this type of essay. The essay is clearly and logically organized into paragraphs, and linking phrases are effective (*E.g. 'Firstly, secondly, overall.'*) The writer uses vocabulary which shows a general understanding of the topic (*E.g. 'Financial transactions, fraudulent loan'*) and the examples given are not excessively regional or detailed. The reader feels that the writer can generate and present ideas clearly and logically.

Example Task 15

Many people today find it difficult to balance the demands of their work and personal life. What are the causes of this situation, and what can individuals and employers do to reduce the problem?

Explanation of the task

Occasionally, an IDEAS task may be a mix of PROBLEM/SOLUTION and CAUSE/EFFECT types. In this example, you are asked to think of some ideas about the causes of a situation, and then propose solutions. You should follow the same structure as for other IDEAS tasks, and give two or three causes, then two or three ideas about solutions (ways to *'reduce the problem'*) and then summarise.

Note that the task requires you to talk about solutions from individuals and also from employers. You should check the task carefully to make sure you have understood any 'extra' requirements such as this. They are quite common in IDEAS type tasks.

Model Essay 15

Finding a compromise between one's job and one's private life is probably harder than ever these days, especially if one has a family. There are several reasons for this, but also a number of measures we can take.

Possibly the major factor is the increased workload that many people have to deal with. The predominance of the service sector means that most people work in office-related jobs, and they find that employers expect them to stay longer or be available outside traditional office hours. On top of this, the rise of communication tools – ranging from smart phones to laptops and teleconferencing equipment – has accelerated the trend, because people are always contactable. Furthermore, the economic recession has made the labour market increasingly competitive, and so workers are under pressure to cooperate in this process, fearing loss of promotion or even redundancy if they resist.

However, there are various steps that can be taken to lessen the problem. Firstly, individuals should clarify with their employer the times when they expect to be free of work and out of contact, thus ensuring private time. Another positive development would be for employers to allow more flexible working hours, so that staff can take time off for important family events during the working day. Lastly, employers could offer advice and coaching to staff in areas such as time management, stress control and relaxation techniques. This would help to reduce the anxiety that stems from heavy workloads and long hours.

In summary, we can say that technology and economics are creating this situation, but also that employees and companies together can reduce the impact.

(268 words)

<u>Examiner's comments</u>

This essay reaches the criteria for band 9. The task is answered fully, with causes and solutions being described, and the writer discusses solutions regarding both individuals and employers. There are three ideas in each section, so the essay feels complete but not too detailed. The introduction guides the reader in what to expect, and the conclusion has a brief but effective summary. The language used is a very high-quality academic style (e.g. *Possibly the major factor, various steps, has accelerated the trend.)* The tone is impersonal and unemotional, while also being persuasive.

Summary of Book One

This completes the fifteen model essays in this book. Please go back and read them again when you have time, paying special attention to the Examiner's Comments which show how the examiners will react to the essay you write. Remember that the examiners can only give you a high mark if you show the following in your essay:

You have analysed and understood the task itself

You make it clear what type of essay you are going to write

You organise the essay into logical paragraphs

You avoid personal emotions and personal stories

Your English is modern and academic, but not too technical or specialised

You use linking phrases to connect the stages of the essay

When you practise writing essays, ask yourself if you are doing these things all the time. By doing this, you can be sure of increasing your chances of achieving the highest grade possible.

Practice Tasks

Here are some are further examples of IELTS Academic Task 2 questions. Try to analyze each one, decide which type of essay it is, and then practice writing an essay in 40 minutes. There is a key on the next page of this book which explains which type each essay is.

Practice Task 1

Some people believe that a person's intelligence is inherited from the parents, while others believe that their environment is the main factor. Discuss these views. Which factor do you think is mostly responsible for intelligence?

Practice Task 2

Playing a musical instrument is one of the most important achievements for any child.

To what extent do you agree with this statement?

Practice Task 3

Analysts tell us that many people today feel stressed and think they have insufficient control over their lives. What problems do such feelings cause for people? What remedies could you suggest?

Practice task 4

It is generally agreed that fewer people today write letters (through the mail or post) compared with the twentieth century. What factors have led to this situation? What will the impact be on the lives of future generations?

Practice Task 5

Governments in many countries are urgently seeking ways to reduce unemployment in rural areas. What are the most effective ways to do this? Which measure do you think would be the single most effective step that governments could take?

Key to Practice Tasks

Practice Task 1 Key: This is an OPINION > DISCUSSION type task.

Practice Task 2 Key: This is an OPINION > PERSONAL VIEWPOINT type task.

Practice Task 3 Key: This is an IDEAS > PROBLEM/SOLUTION type task.

Practice task 4 Key: This is an IDEAS > CAUSE/EFFECT type task.

Practice Task 5 Key: This is an IDEAS > EVALUATE type task.

The 10 most common mistakes in IELTS academic writing

Using contractions (for example *'I don't think'* or *'We can't say')* instead of the full form (*'I do not think'* or *'we cannot say.'*) Never use contractions in academic writing.

Writing too few words. If you write much less than the required word count, the examiner has to reduce your score, even if your essay is good quality. You should count the number of words in your essay after each paragraph and keep a continuous total; this way, you can be sure of reaching at least 250 words in 40 minutes.

Writing too many words. The examiner is paid to mark on an 'essay per hour basis,' and so will not read the end of an essay if it exceeds the minimum word count by more than about 50 words. This means he or she will not see the end of your argument, and your score will reduce considerably. Remember: 250 words minimum, and about 300 words maximum in Academic task 2 writing.

Having handwriting that is difficult to read. Unless you take the new computer-based test, IELTS is still a handwritten exam, and the examiners will not spend much time trying to understand your writing. You must make sure that your handwriting can be read quickly. You should focus on writing clearly when you do your practice essays. Ask friends or other students to give you an honest opinion about whether your writing is easy to read.

Using informal words (for example 'a *nice* idea' or 'a *silly* thing to do') instead of academic words (for example 'a *positive* idea' or 'a *regrettable* thing to do.') Remember that academic vocabulary is different from the language you would use in English when talking to friends.

Giving personal opinion in an IDEAS type task. Check if the task is asking for your opinion or not. The first question you should ask yourself is *'Is this an OPINION or an IDEAS task?'*

Telling stories about your personal history, friends or family. The task tells you to use *'examples from your own experience,'* but this does *not* mean describing stories from your life or people you know. It means describing examples of things in the world that you know about, have studied or have learned about in the media.

Giving evidence which is too detailed or specific to a subject. You may be an expert in a particular social or scientific field, but the examiner probably has a different specialty. You need to make your ideas and examples accessible to a general reader. For example, if the Task topic is about money and you are an accountant, do not use specialized accounting terms.

Being emotional or too dramatic when giving your opinion in an OPINION task. You may feel strongly about issues such as animals or crime, but academic writing must be unemotional. So avoid phrases such as *'a disgusting idea'* or *'I detest this concept.'* It is much better to say *'an unacceptable idea'* or *'I disapprove of this concept,'* which is more impersonal and academic. It is similar to the type of writing that people use in business reports or university essays.

Not following the basic structures presented in this book. The examiners want to see a clear, well-structured essay that is easy to read. They are accustomed to seeing the structures we have presented in this book, and they will feel more positive about your essay if they can recognize these structures in what you write. Remember: the *topic* under discussion will be different every time, but the basic concept behind the task and the essay will be the same. Give the examiners what they want, and they will reward you with a high score, even if there are some grammatical mistakes in your English.

BOOK TWO
IELTS Vocabulary Secrets

Book Two: IELTS Vocabulary Secrets

Introduction to Book Two

There are two parts of the IELTS exam in which the test asks some questions and you must create independent responses: the Speaking Test and the Writing Test. Many people do not realise that the IELTS system uses a group of ten key topics to formulate all of these questions in Speaking and Writing. If you understand these ten topics, and above all if you know some advanced vocabulary on each topic to use in your Speaking and Writing answers, you can make a huge difference to your IELTS Band score, even if your English contains some mistakes.

This book introduces you to these ten IELTS topics. They are:

1. Work and careers
2. Education and schooling
3. Children and families
4. Nature, the environment and energy
5. Culture, art and traditions
6. Healthcare, health and sport
7. Global challenges
8. Cities and infrastructure
9. The countryside and agriculture
10. Government and the authorities

Each of our ten modules summarises the various elements of a topic, and gives an example Academic Task 2 Writing Task exactly like the ones you will see in the exam. It also explains how to answer the writing Task. Each module then teaches a large amount of vocabulary related to the module topic, contained in a Band 9 model essay so that you see how the words are used in IELTS writing. Each module has a clear-to-follow definition of each word or phrase, and a further example of how to use these topic words again in the Speaking part of the test, so that you are ready to use the vocabulary in both Writing and Speaking.

This book will teach you a very large amount of vocabulary of exactly the type that the IELTS examiners want to read and hear from you in the exam, covering the ten IELTS topics. It is important that you prepare to answer questions on *all* of these ten topics, because they all may be used in the test. Therefore, don't start by trying to remember absolutely all the words from Module 1, then all the words from Module 2 and so on. Try to learn and practise a small number of words from Modules 1 to 10 at first, and then a slightly larger group of words from

Modules 1 to 10, and so on. This will help you develop a wide IELTS vocabulary on all the topics, and not become a 'specialist' in just one topic.

If you are not yet familiar with the different parts of the IELTS Speaking test, please consider reading our e-book *Get IELTS Band 9 in Speaking.* If you need a dictionary while using this book, we recommend the free *Cambridge Dictionaries Online* from Cambridge University Press. Don't just trust to luck in your IELTS exam – the key is expert advice!

Jessica Alperne & Peter Swires

Frequently Asked Questions About the IELTS Vocabulary Topics

Why does the IELTS exam use these ten topics all the time?

The IELTS test managers believe that these topics are the most suited to advanced, academic discussion in the world today, and also that people who take IELTS should have a reasonable understanding and interest regarding these areas.

I see that one Topic is about 'Agriculture,' for example. I know little about this, even in my native language. Is this a problem?

No! Remember that in IELTS Speaking and Academic Writing, you are not expected to know specialised technical words or understand complex issues. The vocabulary expected is what a normal person can meet when reading the media, newspapers, popular websites and magazines on these subjects. Don't worry if you think some of these topics seem too advanced – the vocabulary that we show you will enable you to answer questions in these areas quite easily, with some practice.

Do I need to remember all of the words in this book?

You should try to remember a group of words on each topic, and practise using them in your writing and speaking. People have different styles of memory, of course. We believe that a typical IELTS candidate should be able to learn and use at least ten new words and phrases for each of the ten topics. This should make a massive difference to the strength of your IELTS Writing and Speaking.

Will this book also help me with the Reading and Listening IELTS tests?

Yes, because the ten topics are also used to formulate the Reading and Listening materials. The Reading and Listening papers will additionally contain some quite specialised vocabulary, but the IELTS tests are carefully designed so that you should be able to get a high band even if you don't know this more specialised language.

Topic 1: Work and Careers

About Topic 1

The work and careers topic includes issues of opportunities and problems at work, ways of motivating and rewarding workers, the work/life balance, changes in patterns of jobs and work (for example, the growth in working from home,) career choices and training, and occasionally the relationship between government and business or industries.

You are not expected to know any vocabulary connected to specialised areas of finance, marketing and so on.

Topic 1 Example Task

Some employers offer their employees subsidised membership of gyms and sports clubs, believing that this will make their staff healthier and thus more effective at work. Other employers see no benefit in doing so.

Consider the arguments from both aspects of this possible debate, and reach a conclusion.

Explanation of the Task

This is an Opinion > Discussion type Task. You should introduce the topic, present two or three ideas on each side of the discussion, and then give your opinion in the conclusion.

The following model essay shows you key words and phrases which you can use to increase your band score when discussing this topic, in both writing and speaking. The key words are **highlighted in bold**.

Band 9 model essay

Employers are always seeking ways to enhance their employees' **productivity**, and **subsidising** healthy pursuits may be one way of achieving this. There are arguments on both sides, however, which we will discuss here.

On the one hand, it might be said that if workers are fitter and less stressed, their working time will be more efficient, leading to higher levels of **output** and service. Furthermore, the **work/life balance** of the staff will hopefully be improved, because their leisure time will be more fulfilling. This may even be more **motivating** than **pay increments, perks,** or **financial rewards** such as **bonuses** or **incentives** which may be hard to attain. Finally, feeling healthier may lead to better **job satisfaction** which is in itself a motivating factor.

Conversely, the problem with such leisure-based subsidies is that their efficacy is virtually impossible to quantify. For example, with **target-related** payments, employers can at least see whether the objectives are reached or not. It might also be said that, if this budget was spent on (for instance) **on the job training** or **day release programmes**, the employees would achieve better **career progression** and have better **job prospects.** These matters are all easier to **measure**, especially in **performance reviews** and **appraisals,** and may even help to reduce the risk of **redundancy** if the company **restructures, downsizes** or **outsources** its **workforce.**

Overall, it seems that, while health-related subsidies are **superficially** attractive, the lack of **measurability** is a substantial drawback. Spending funds on **ongoing training** would appear to be a better use of company or **Human Resources** budgets.

(259 words)

Explanation of the topic vocabulary and examples of use in the Speaking Test

These words and phrases are listed in the order that they appear in the essay. Please remember that these extra example sentences are designed to show you ways of using this vocabulary in IELTS Speaking, and so the examples may include contractions (*'don't'* etc) and personal stories about the speaker and their family or friends. This is fine in the Speaking test, but not in Task 2 writing, which should never have contractions or personal stories.

These Speaking examples also sometimes include less formal words such as 'really' or 'good.' Again, these words are acceptable in Speaking, but try to use more formal words in Writing, such as 'substantially' or 'positive.'

productivity = the ability of people to produce useful results at work.

Example of using this vocabulary item in the IELTS Speaking Test:

My country is not as advanced as some other countries in our industrial sector. Productivity and quality are still quite low.

to subsidise = to pay part of the cost of something, usually in order to help people.

The government could encourage children to be healthier by subsidising swimming lessons and sports coaching at weekends.

output = the amount of work or goods produced.

In Europe, industrial output has decreased, maybe because of competition from producers in other continents.

work/life balance = the ability to work hard but also enjoy a good quality family and social life.

People are working long hours these days, and so their work/life balance is affected, leading to stress.

to motivate people = to give them positive reasons for working hard.

If employees are given regular feedback, they will probably be well motivated and committed.

pay increments = pay rises/increases.

In my country, pay increments have been very low because of the financial crisis.

perks = rewards from an employer which are not financial (e.g. free lunches, a car etc.)

Personally, I'd like to work for a company that gives lots of perks, because I would find this very enjoyable.

financial rewards = any form of money payment (salary, commission, pension etc.)

Being a primary teacher may be satisfying, but the financial rewards are not high.

bonuses = money given in addition to salary, usually in return for achieving targets.

Apparently, some investment bankers can earn millions of dollars in bonuses.

incentives = any reward that makes people work harder.

Some employers offer vacations or parties as incentives if the team hits its sales targets.

job satisfaction = enjoyment of a job for non-financial reasons

I get a lot of job satisfaction from my work at the wildlife centre, although the financial rewards are quite low.

target-related = dependent on hitting a target.

My boss once offered me a target-related bonus, but it was almost impossible to achieve!

on the job training = training while working, not by leaving work to go to college etc.

My sister has found that the on the job training she gets at her bank is very useful, and she has progressed well because of this.

ongoing training = training throughout your time in a job, not just at the start.

I enjoyed my work at the airline at first, but I soon found that there was no ongoing training and my skills weren't really developed.

day release programmes = programmes of training or education when employees can spend entire days out of work.

I feel that employers should be much more flexible regarding training, for example by subsidising day release programmes or job exchanges with other companies.

career progression = the ability to advance your career.

The problem with being a freelance photographer is that there's no real career progression, unless you become very famous.

job prospects = the possibility of promotion or higher-level work in future.

I remember an interview when the employer told me there were excellent job prospects in their firm for young people. In reality, this was not really true.

to measure = to assess the dimensions of something.

Job satisfaction may be important, but can we really measure it?

superficial = not addressing deep or important issues.

I'm not a big fan of traditional music. I find the lyrics rather old-fashioned and superficial for modern listeners.

performance reviews/appraisals = meeting at which an employer gives feedback to a worker on their work over a fixed period.

I remember being worried about my job at first, but at my six month appraisal my manager told me she was fairly pleased with my efforts.

redundancy = a situation where a worker loses their job because of changes in the company (not because of personal mistakes) (verb = to make someone redundant.)

In my home town, the textile factories have closed and many people have been made redundant.

to restructure = to change the organisation of a company, usually in order to make it more effective or to save money.

We used to have a large training department in my office, but in our recent restructure it was eliminated and the staff were made redundant.

to downsize = to make an organisation smaller and employ fewer people.

My mother's college used to employ almost one thousand people, but then it downsized and now has less than five hundred.

to outsource = to stop doing work inside the company and send it to other companies or other countries, usually to save money.

Many American companies have outsourced their IT operations to Asian countries, where productivity is similar and salaries are lower.

the workforce = the total number of people working in an organisation, company or country

The workforce in Northern Europe is skilled, but it's also inflexible and much older than in other parts of the world.

Human Resources (or HR**)** = the department in a company which manages recruitment, employment and training.

When I graduate, I plan to work in the Human Resources area of the oil industry, possibly in the Middle East.

Summary of Topic 1

This completes our Module for Topic 1.

Remember, please don't try to learn or memorise *all* of these words immediately. Go through the whole book from Module 1 to 10, and try to practise using a small group of words from each of the Modules, then go back and expand your control of each group.

Topic 2: Education and Schooling

About Topic 2

The education and schooling topic includes teaching methods and resources, approaches to exams and testing, school management, pupil motivation, behaviour and discipline, school sport, extra-curricular activities, higher/further education and course funding.

Topic 2 example Task

'The Internet will never replace traditional course books in schools.'
How far do you agree with this prediction?

Explanation of the Task

This is an Opinion > Personal viewpoint type essay (it asks how far you agree with an idea.) You should introduce the topic and give your opinion in the introduction, then explain why you have this view. You should briefly consider the opposing view, then restate your opinion in the conclusion.

Notice how this essay type is different from the Opinion > Discussion type which we saw in Topic 1, which asks you to *discuss* both sides of a debate.

Band 9 model essay

There is a huge range of resources available to the modern teacher, and the right selection is crucial in delivering effective lessons. I agree that there will always be a place for course books in the school **curriculum**, despite the many benefits of the Internet.

Firstly, course books (whether conventional or digital) have been developed by **pedagogical** experts and designed to be incorporated into a subject **syllabus,** leading to testing procedures such as **formal examinations** or **continuous assessment**. This means that they are proven to improve students' **academic achievement**, enhancing their potential for progression to **further** or **higher education.** Furthermore, the use of modern course books allows pupils to coordinate their studies as part of **group work**, hopefully making their lessons less **teacher-led** and more about **autonomous learning**. This in itself teaches **study skills** such as independent research and **synthesising sources**, rather than old-fashioned **rote-learning.** This is where the Internet, in fact, can play a useful part: to **supplement** and add to **knowledge** which the students are **assimilating** via their course books. However, it is the role of teachers and school management generally to ensure that use of the Internet remains a **guided learning** process, and not an exercise in **data-gathering** from Internet sources which may be unreliable or even misleading.

It is true that the Internet can be invaluable for adults (for example in **distance learning** or **self-study** modules) who are able to **discriminate between sources** and **sift information** to **marshal their facts**. However, this is a mature skill and we should not assume that school age pupils are ready to do this.

Overall, it appears that course books, with their quality and depth of material, are set to remain **an integral part of the syllabus**. The internet can be judged a useful supplement to this, if used carefully and **under supervision**.

(304 words)

<u>Explanation of the topic vocabulary and examples in speaking</u>

curriculum = the full range of subjects offered by a school or group of schools.

The curriculum in private schools is sometimes wider than in state schools, because they have more resources.

pedagogical (experts) = (experts in) education and teaching.

I admire pedagogical pioneers such as the Scandinavian thinkers who began free schools for all children.

syllabus = the content of elements taught in a specific subject.

The syllabus for geography at my school included volcanoes, earthquakes and tidal waves, which we found fascinating.

formal examinations = exams where students answer set written or spoken questions without assistance.

continuous assessment = giving students marks for course work or projects, rather than formal exams.

At my school, our grades were based 50/50 on formal examinations and continuous assessment, which we thought was very fair to all the children.

academic achievement = the measurable performance of a student in marks, exam results etc.

In my country, children enjoy school, and so academic achievement is quite high.

further education = education after leaving school at the minimum age.

Some governments encourage further education by allowing teenagers to claim benefits while they study.

higher education = education after age 18 at college or University, usually for a degree.

When I pass IELTS, I plan to go on to higher education in Canada and do a degree in engineering.

group work = study where pupils discuss and agree a project together.

Personally, I think that group work enables lazy children to do less work than the eager ones.

teacher-led lessons = traditional lessons where the teacher delivers a long talk and the students take notes.

In my country, lessons are still very teacher-led and interaction is rather limited.

autonomous learning = when a student learns through independent study and research.

At University, you are expected to be an autonomous learner far more than at High School, which is quite exciting for me.

study skills = the skills of organising, using and checking study work.

My study skills were rather weak until I read an excellent book by a Japanese pedagogical expert.

to synthesise sources = to use a variety of sources and combine them in one project.

I use the Internet to synthesise my sources, and I always cite the origin of the information (to cite sources = to acknowledge publicly.)

rote-learning = learning by repetition and memorising items.

I used to think that rote-learning was a negative approach, but my recent experiences teaching in a South African school have changed my view.

to supplement = to add extra content or material.

My supervisor said that I should supplement my essay with more examples of experiments.

to assimilate knowledge = to absorb and understand it.

I always use a dictionary when I study in English, to help me assimilate new phrases.

guided learning = learning under the supervision of a teacher.

Lessons in Primary Schools should always contain guided learning, otherwise the children will lose focus.

data-gathering = collecting information, usually in numerical form.

Mobile phone companies employ many people in data-gathering Tasks, to see how users are using the phones and Internet.

distance learning = learning by the Internet or email, rather than face-to-face.

My mother took an entire degree by distance learning over a period of five years.

self-study = studying using a course without a teacher's involvement.

There are many self-study guides to improving your English, and some of them are actually quite good.

to discriminate between sources = to decide whether one source is better or more reliable than another source.

Children should not study using unsupervised Internet access, because they can't discriminate between the sources of information they find.

to sift information = to remove unwanted or less useful information.

I had to sift hundreds of pages of data to arrive at my conclusions when I did my thesis.

to marshal facts = to organise facts in support of an idea.

In IELTS essays, you should marshal a few facts to support each idea in the argument.

an integral part of the syllabus = essential, central or indispensable.

Nutrition is an integral part of food sciences these days.

to work/study under supervision = under the direction of a responsible person.

At college, I discovered I did not have to work under supervision all the time, and I was free to do independent research.

Topic 3: Children and Families

About Topic 3

The children and families topic includes child psychology and development, ways of bringing up children, family discipline, child care, preschool learning, parental roles, family structures and roles (for example nuclear or extended families) adolescence, teenagers and elderly family members.

Please remember that the topics are used in different ways in the Writing and Speaking parts of the IELTS test.

In the Academic Writing test Task 2, you should present ideas or opinions about society in general, but not about your personal life. In the Speaking test, the examiner will always ask you both about society in general (in Speaking part 3) and also about your personal life, country and background (in Speaking parts 1 and 2.)

With controversial topics such as 'families' and 'health,' some candidates become confused about this difference, but it's absolutely essential to remember if you want to achieve a very high band score.

Topic 3 example Task

Some people believe that children should spend all of their free time with their families. Others believe that this is unnecessary or even negative. Discuss the possible arguments on both sides, and say which side you personally support.

Explanation of the Task

This is another Opinion>Discussion type Task. You should introduce the topic, present two or three ideas on each side of the discussion, and then give your opinion in the conclusion. Remember that these Opinion>Discussion Tasks might be expressed in different ways; look for the instruction key word 'discuss' and its synonyms such as 'debate,' 'consider' and 'review.'

Band 9 model essay

Nobody can deny that parental influence is important for children, at least in cases where children live with their parents, **foster parents** or **guardians**. However, it is by no means clear that children should spend time exclusively in the family, as we will see.

On the one hand, it may appear advisable for parents to act as **role models** and to establish **ground rules** for behaviour by spending as much time as possible with their children. This allows the youngsters to **absorb conventions** and **codes of conduct** which they can then follow themselves, hopefully leading to an absence of problems such as **bullying, truancy** and **delinquency** later on. Furthermore, being with the family should reduce the risk of children falling victim to crimes such as **abduction**, or coming under the influence of negative **peer pressure.**

On the other hand, we have to ask whether this is a practical proposition. In a society where many families are **dual-income**, or where one parent's role as **breadwinner** means he/she is away from the family for long periods, it is inevitable that children cannot spend all of their time with the family. **Child-minding** and **after-school childcare** are often used in these cases, and if managed properly, these can be perfectly **viable** alternatives. Equally, it seems that children can in some cases learn a considerable amount from their **peers** in addition to adults, and allowing them to play without direct supervision may be a benefit.

To conclude, it appears that, while family time is essential for **bonding** and **absorbing patterns of behaviour**, there are definite advantages when children are outside the family too. This is provided that they are in a safe, well-behaved environment with peers who are themselves reasonably **well brought-up**.

(287 words)

Explanation of the topic vocabulary and examples in speaking

foster parents = people who have children living in their existing family for a fixed period, with the agreement of the parents or the authorities.

Being a foster parent is a difficult and tiring role, I can imagine.

guardians = people who are legally appointed to protect a child's interests in the absence of parents.

In some countries, the government appoints a guardian if the parents die or experience severe difficulties.

role models = people that children look to and respect as good examples.

In some countries, the royal family are good role models for youngsters, although in other cases this is not the case.

ground rules = basic rules governing the way people can behave in a situation.

During the school holidays, my parents had strict ground rules for what we could do outside.

conventions = traditions or social norms that most people follow.

It's a convention for grandparents to live with their children in many countries.

codes of conduct = voluntary rules which people accept in a situation.

The Boy Scouts have a firm code of conduct, which seems to be a positive influence.

bullying = when children attack and intimidate other children.

Bullying could be reduced through better awareness and positive peer pressure in schools.

truancy = when a pupil leaves school without permission (verb = to play truant from school.)

I must confess that at secondary school I sometimes played truant and went to the park with my friends.

delinquency = minor crime (often by young people.)

Delinquency is a huge problem in urban areas, especially when policing is minimal.

abduction = the crime of taking or kidnapping people for a criminal reason.

Child abduction is a great concern for many parents, especially in South America.

peer pressure = the pressure from people in the same group to act in a certain wa.y

Many children start smoking due to peer pressure or bad role models.

dual-income = a family where both the father and mother work.

In many countries, the dual-income family is the norm nowadays.

breadwinner = the person who earns all or most of the money in a family.

In some families, the father is still the only breadwinner.

child-minding = caring informally (not in schools) for children when parents are busy or working.

In some countries, the state subsidises the costs of child-minding.

after-school childcare = caring for children in a school setting, as above.

Many families rely on after-school childcare because both parents work and commute.

viable = practical and possible to achieve.

It is not really viable to expect all children to get maximum grades in exams.

peers = people in the same group or level as yourself.

Many of my peers from school are now working for charities.

bonding = the development of close emotional connections between people.

Festivals and parties are an ideal time for families to bond.

patterns of behaviour = ways of acting and doing things (either positive or negative.)

Unfortunately, some children absorb dangerous patterns of behaviour when watching movies or playing computer games.

well brought-up = raised as a child to have good manners (to bring up children = to raise and educate them in your own moral, behavioural or religious conventions.)

I was brought up in a very religious family, and I seem to have absorbed their values.

Topic 4: Nature, Environment and Energy

About Topic 4

The nature, environment and energy topic includes fossil fuels and renewable fuels, climate change, threats to the environment (deforestation, pollution etc) and their effects, the biosphere, and animal life/human attitudes to animals.

In this topic, remember to show that you can write in an impersonal, academic way, even if you feel strongly about something. Remember that emotional words such as *terrible, shocking, disgusting* or *wonderful, fantastic, brilliant* cannot be used in Academic English essays of this type. You can use Academic English such as *regrettable, worrying, inadvisable* or *admirable, helpful, invaluable* instead, which are more accepted in these situations.

This topic is often used for Ideas > Cause/effect type Tasks.

Topic 4 example Task

Pollution of rivers, lakes and seas is a major concern for people who seek to protect the environment. What are the possible causes of water pollution, and what effects does this have on animal life and human society?

Explanation of the Task

This is an Ideas > Cause/effect type Task. It does not ask for your opinion, but it wants you to think of some possible ideas on the topic. You should introduce the topic, describe two or three causes, then two or three effects, and then summarise briefly.

Band 9 model essay

Water **contamination** is a serious form of pollution, and one that can be challenging to rectify. There seem to be two main causes involved, and a variety of damaging effects on people and **the biosphere**, which we will discuss here.

Probably the main factor is the issue of **emissions** from cars, factories and other human activities. These emissions contain damaging **pollutant particles** which can contaminate rainwater **run-off** and thus enter **the water cycle**, by transferring through the water table into **aquifers**, streams and rivers. **Filtration** and processing are not really viable options for such large volumes of water, and so the **water table** remains **tainted** with these elements over long periods, as we see in Eastern Europe today. In situations where **soil erosion** and **logging** have already damaged the local environment, the accumulation can be very serious. The other major cause is accidental or deliberate **dumping** of **waste** products in places outside of controlled **landfills** or **waste processing** centres. Even small amounts of abandoned waste can enter water supplies through the ground, often undetected.

The effects on animal life can be severe, especially for species which are already endangered by such threats as **poaching, habitat loss** and **food chain** disruption. Contaminated water can lead to **dwindling numbers** or even potential **extinction**, as may indeed happen to the Asian tiger populations. The impact on human society can also be distressing, including the poisoning of drinking water, **famine** or **drought** due to lack of safe **irrigation**, and long-term loss of land as we see, for example, after the Bhopal poisoning **catastrophe** in India. Such effects tend to have an especially grave impact on the very poorest in society, with the least resources to counter the environmental effects.

Overall, we see that emissions and dumping are the main origins of the problem, and that the effects on both humans and animals are **exacerbated** by the existing environmental, criminal or social problems.

(316 words)

<u>Explanation of the topic vocabulary and examples in speaking</u>

contamination = pollution by poisons or dangerous elements.

The atmosphere in large cities is often contaminated by smog, as we can see in China.

the biosphere = the relationship between all living things on the planet.

Children should be educated on the biosphere through field trips and practical experiments.

emissions = gases entering the atmosphere.

Scientists spend their whole careers studying the effect of emissions on the climate.

pollutant particles = microscopic elements of pollution.

I remember going to a factory and seeing the snow covered with pollutant particles.

run-off = water that runs from the ground into rivers and lakes.

We should try to collect and use more run-off water, to avoid having to recycle water so much.

the water cycle = the natural process of water moving from clouds to rain and seas.

Scientists believe the water cycle is responsible for various natural events, especially in coastal areas.

aquifers = underground, natural water stores.

My family have a well which connects to an aquifer, giving very pure water.

filtration = the process of filtering and removing impurities.

Water filtration might be a solution to water shortages in very hot countries.

water table = the layer of water below ground.

In my town, the water table is very high, and water will appear in even a small hole.

tainted = polluted or contaminated.

The Mediterranean is badly tainted in some areas by sewage pollution.

soil erosion = the loss of soil by wind and rain activity.

Deforestation has increased soil erosion seriously in Brazil.

logging = cutting down trees for timber and industrial use.

Logging has endangered many species throughout the world.

dumping = leaving waste deliberately without storing or treating it.

In most countries, dumping rubbish is a criminal offence.

waste = any material not wanted or needed after a process.

In my country, we use waste from cotton manufacture for lighting fires.

landfills = organised areas where waste is buried in the ground.

Surprisingly, Britain still sends most of its domestic waste to landfill sites.

waste processing = recycling or reducing waste into manageable forms.

My brother has a waste processing company, which is subsidised by the local authority.

poaching = illegally hunting and killing animals.

Elephant poaching should be a much higher priority for the world authorities, as elephants are an endangered species.

habitat loss = destruction or disappearance of an animal's natural home.

Logging has caused substantial habitat loss for wildlife in many countries.

food chain = the natural system of animals eating other animals and plants.

The food chain has been disrupted by the loss of certain species, with widespread impacts on all animals.

dwindling numbers = (to dwindle = to steadily decline in quantity.)

States seem to have dwindling funds to pay for animal sanctuaries, although they are still able to pay for government officials and their perks.

extinction = the final death of all animals in a species.

Dinosaur extinction may have been caused by a meteor or volcano, but scientists seem unsure about this.

famine = a situation where there is a lack of food in an area for a long time.

Many singers help make charity songs to raise funds for famine relief.

drought = similar to famine, but a lack of water.

Drought in central Africa can continue for many years.

irrigation = supplying water to land for agriculture.

If we want quick solutions to famine, better irrigation and farming methods would probably be the first step.

catastrophe = a great disaster affecting many people.

The continuing destruction of the rain forests is a catastrophe for the global biosphere.

exacerbated (= to exacerbate = to make an existing problem worse, accidentally or deliberately.)

Famine in Africa has been exacerbated by civil war and political instability.

Topic 5: Culture, Art and Traditions

About Topic 5

The culture, art and traditions topic includes human folklore, ceremonies and rituals, myths and legends, social customs, traditional languages, dress and arts, the impact of modern life on traditional lifestyles and differences in national habits.

Please remember that IELTS will not ask specifically about religion, politics or spiritual beliefs, and you should not base your answers in the Writing or Speaking tests on your personal beliefs in these areas. For example, if the Task asks whether you agree with a certain idea, you would get a low mark if you say *'Yes, because my religion agrees with it/because my President has this policy'* or similar.

You can certainly use religious or political situations as evidence or examples to support an argument, but not as a starting point. For example, *'We should give money to charity because it benefits society, as we can see for example in countries where religious observance requires people to do this regularly.'* This is a more logical and academic way to respond.

Topic 5 example Task

In many countries, traditional dress and costumes are considered effective ways of maintaining links with the past. How effective can traditional costumes be, in this sense?

What other ways exist to help citizens connect with a country's past?

Explanation of the Task

This is an Ideas > Evaluate type essay.

It does not ask for your opinion about whether costumes are good or bad, but it asks for you to decide whether these costumes are effective (or not effective) ways of maintaining links with the past, and to suggest other ways of connecting to the past. You should say how effective costumes are, with examples and evidence, and then compare their effectiveness to some other possible ways of connecting to the past.

Remember that 'Ideas > Evaluate' means that you should compare things in the way that they are used in society, but not decide on your personal preference about these things.

Band 9 model essay

Most people would agree that **preserving** connections with our past is an admirable objective, especially as the world evolves so rapidly. I feel that traditional costumes are one part of doing this, but they are by no means the most important, as we shall see.

Admittedly, historic dress plays a key role in social events such as religious **rituals** or military **parades**, and these events are helpful in **transmitting social memes** such as **public duty** and **self-sacrifice.** Traditional costumes also remind us of the origins of **cultural traditions and mythologies**, for instance the historic Swiss national dress which **evokes** their **medieval** independence.

However, it must be said that costumes are an accessory in these situations, and do not appear to constitute the central message. It is the **ceremonies** themselves which convey the **cultural norms** that help to maintain **the fabric of society.** In this sense, the costumes are of secondary importance. Furthermore, it seems that there are in fact much more powerful ways in which culture is **conserved** and **handed down** between the generations. Most countries have a rich **heritage** of **legends** and **folklore** about the birth and development of their nation, some of which are mythological and some being grounded in truth (as we see in the English stories about Robin Hood or George and the Dragon, for example.) These stories are a **cultural inheritance** which embodies important symbols and concepts far more effectively than dress. Similarly, we must remember the significance of art and music in passing on our traditions, in **forms** ranging from **fine art** to **handicrafts**, and from **opera** to traditional **shanties** and **dirges.** The presence of visual or **linguistic** messages in these **media** make them more effective than costumes, which convey no language.

Overall, we must recognise and welcome the use of traditional dress in helping to maintain our cultures. However, the forms of story, art and music would appear to be the driving forces in this invaluable process.

(321 words)

Explanation of the topic vocabulary and examples in speaking

to preserve = to protect and keep something, usually because it is valuable for some reason.

The state preserves ancient buildings because they are part of our heritage.

rituals = highly traditional ceremonies which have meaning for the participants.

In some countries, wedding rituals continue for several days.

parades = organised processions in public by groups of people, usually to commemorate an event.

In my home town, we have a military parade each year to mark our Independence Day.

to transmit = to communicate a message, literal or symbolic.

The monarchy transmits symbols of power through dress and ritual.

social memes = social habits or patterns which are transmitted between people.

In Britain, punctuality is a social meme.

public duty = the willingness to serve the public or the state.

Civil servants need a sense of public duty.

self-sacrifice = the willingness to suffer or die for a cause.

We remember the self-sacrifice of our wartime generation each year.

cultural traditions = traditions carrying cultural importance.

Hospitality is a great cultural tradition in Mediterranean countries.

mythology, myth = a classic story from the past which people know is not true but which carries meaning.

There are old myths about gigantic animals in my part of the countryside.

to evoke = to bring back memories or feelings.

Our national flag evokes strong emotions whenever we see it.

medieval = adjective for the Middle Ages, roughly 1050 to 1400 in European history.

France has some superb medieval architecture, which I saw on my gap year.

ceremonies = a ceremony is similar to a ritual, usually involving people in authority.

The government enters office with a long ceremony at the presidential palace.

cultural norms = standards expected of behaviour or ideas.

In some countries, marriage between cousins is a cultural norm.

the fabric of society = the way that society is connected and maintained.

Drugs and crime are damaging the fabric of society.

to conserve = a synonym for 'to preserve.'

Conservation of old treasures is the main role of our city museum.

to hand something down (from one generation to the next) = to pass it from parents to children and to their children etc.

Cultural values have been handed down for hundreds of years, but now they are starting to disappear.

heritage = something inherited (= received/handed down) by one generation from the previous generation.

Our countryside is part of our national heritage and we should preserve it carefully.

legends = similar to myths, but sometimes containing an element of reality.

Robin Hood is a British legend, although most historians agree the character is based on a real person.

folklore = old stories and myths/legends, usually transmitted verbally.

African folklore is rich in stories of gods and monsters.

inheritance = a synonym for 'heritage.'

Our greatest inheritance as a nation is our independence and fighting spirit.

fine art = art by famous or acclaimed painters.

Florence in Italy is a key destination for lovers of fine art.

handicrafts = skills of making objects by hand, and also the objects themselves.

Many indigenous people make a living by selling handicrafts to tourists.

opera = a very formal play with a musical score.

La Scala is the name of a famous opera venue in Italy, which I'd like to visit.

shanties and **dirges =** very traditional songs about basic subjects.

Children sometimes sing shanties at primary school.

linguistic = the adjective meaning 'about language'

Linguistic skills are essential for a tour guide in the modern economy.

A medium (media = plural) = a way of communicating.

Folklore is a very effective medium for transmitting our cultural heritage.

(The phrase 'the media' is used to mean all the newspapers, broadcasters, websites and magazines commenting on issues in a country: *The president resigned due to pressure from the media, who disliked his policies.*)

Topic 6: Healthcare, Health and Sport

About the topic

The healthcare, health and sport topic includes health problems and disabilities (physical and mental), ways of keeping fit and healthy, diet/nutrition and exercise, ways of providing (and educating people about) healthcare and health services, medical innovations and treatments, and the benefits and management of common sports.

This is one topic especially where you need to remember *not* to give personal stories about yourself or people that you know in the Task 2 Writing.

Topic 3 example Task

Many doctors are concerned about the high use of computer games by children and young people. What mental and physical problems may arise from excessive use of these games? How could these problems be reduced?

Explanation of the Task

This is an Ideas > Problem/solution type Task.

It does not ask about whether computer games are good or not, but about your ideas regarding possible mental and physical problems due to excessive use, and also any solutions that you can think of.

You should introduce the topic, describe two or three problems, then two or three solutions, and then summarise. Notice that the Task asks about mental and physical problems, so you should say something on each type of problem.

Band 9 model essay

Children appear to enjoy playing video games, and while there are undoubted benefits, various negative effects **stem** from this too. Let us consider the main issues, and then outline possible remedies.

Perhaps the major physical problem is the **sedentary lifestyle** which these games encourage, meaning that youngsters may incline to **obesity** or **inadequate development.** Added to this is the **strain** on eyesight resulting from excessive use of screens and consoles, meaning that children may suffer **symptoms** of poor vision. There are also concerns about **impairment** of reflexes due to the repetitive nature of the hand muscles when playing these games, and about the **poor diet** of **convenience food** which often accompanies this lifestyle.

The most alarming psychological impact of such activities is possibly the risk of **addiction**, meaning that children become obsessed with the games and are unable to **socialise** with family or peers. This undermines their **interpersonal skills** and makes them **underperform** both academically and socially.

Turning to possible solutions, perhaps the immediate step would be to promote a more **active lifestyle** through exercise **regimes** or sports **programmes** which would help to **detoxify** the lifestyles of children affected. This could be done through **sponsorship** of sports, or **participation** in **competitive** events such as races or matches, hopefully **ameliorating the physical effects** of excessive games use. Potential **remedies** for the danger of mental addiction may be, firstly, an **initiative** to **raise awareness** of the risks of the situation, for example through **health warnings** on games packaging or through high-profile spokespersons spreading such a message. For example, if sports **champions** or **figureheads** speak out about these dangers, the message may well get through to children.

To sum up, the risks posed by excessive gaming are connected to an unhealthy lifestyle and the possibility of **dependency** on the activity. Possible answers might involve stronger education about the dangers and the health benefits of more active **pursuits**.

(313 words)

<u>Explanation of the topic vocabulary and examples in speaking</u>

to stem from = to come or derive from, often used for negative things.

A lot of delinquency these days stems from the use of drugs or alcohol.

sedentary lifestyle = a lifestyle where people sit for long periods and are generally inactive.

I used to keep fit, but since I started working as an architect my lifestyle had become mostly sedentary.

obesity = the medical condition of being seriously overweight.

In some countries, obesity is the major cause of death among young adults.

inadequate development = insufficient or obstructed growth of the body.

If children smoke, this can cause inadequate development of their lungs and brains.

strain = stress or overwork, physical or mental.

I had to take a vacation due to the strain of working such long hours.

symptoms = indications that a medical problem is present.

A sore throat and headache are symptoms of a cold or flu.

impairment (verb = to impair = to hinder or damage an ability.)

His hearing was impaired when he heard a loud explosion as a child.

poor diet = a pattern of eating without sufficient nutrients.

Malnutrition happens due to a poor diet and lack of medical care.

('a diet' can also mean a programme of reduced calories intended to help you lose weight: *'My sister is always trying new diets because she wants to lose 2 kilos before the summer.'*)

convenience food = food which is cooked in its packaging, usually in a microwave.

British and American people eat a large amount of convenience food.

addiction = the state of being unable to live without something.

Many young people are addicted to social media or Internet use.

to socialise = to meet with friends and other people in a friendly way.

At weekends, I like to socialise at parties and in cafes with my old friends.

interpersonal skills = the skills of dealing with people successfully.

My boss used to be very annoying, but then he went on a course to develop proper interpersonal skills.

to underperform = to perform below your peers or expectations.

My football team are underperforming badly this year.

active lifestyle = a lifestyle with proper exercise and fitness.

The government tries to promote an active lifestyle, but this is not successful.

a regime, a programme = a planned system of exercise, diet or sport.

I adopted a vegetarian regime for three months before my exams.

('regime' also means a very strict government: *'In the 1970's, many South American countries were ruled by police regimes.'*)

to detoxify your body = to remove impurities and poisons.

I went to a clinic to detoxify because I was eating too much fatty food.

sponsorship = payment from a company to a sport or other activity in return for publicity.

Motor racing is often sponsored by energy drink brands.

participation (noun) (to participate in something = verb) = to join and take part in it.

I participated in wrestling when I was at college, but then I gave up.

competitive = the adjective of 'competition.'

Canadians are very competitive about ice hockey teams.

ameliorating the physical effects = to ameliorate = to make a problem less damaging.

The effects of his injury were ameliorated by extensive physiotherapy.

remedies = cures or answers to a problem or situation.

There are many remedies for cold and flu available in pharmacy stores.

an initiative = a new programme or idea, usually in government or business.

We need initiatives to tackle obesity, anti-social behaviour and delinquency.

raise awareness = to make people more aware of or caring about an issue.

We organised a marathon to raise awareness of heart disease and ways to prevent it through exercise.

health warnings = notices on cigarette or alcohol packaging warning about the medical effects.

Almost all countries have health warnings on tobacco these days.

champions = highly successful people in sport or business.

Roger Federer is a champion tennis player, and a good role model too.

figureheads = people who represent part of society, officially or unofficially.

The singer Adele is a figurehead for many young women these days.

dependency = the condition of relying on something in an addictive way.

The player was treated for drug dependency at a detox clinic in Paris.

pursuits = hobbies or sports which people do for enjoyment

Skiing and cycling are my main pursuits at weekends.

Topic 7: Global Challenges

About Topic 7

The global challenges topic includes economic issues, their impact on people and society, changes in demographics, movements of populations between countries and inside countries, long term trends in population and industry, severe global problems such as famine, drought and malnutrition, and also the possible causes of all these issues, their effects and possible solutions to them.

There are often connections between this topic and the other topics, especially

4 Nature, Environment and Energy, 8 Cities and Infrastructure, 9 The Countryside and Agriculture, and 10 Government and the Authorities. This means that you may sometimes need to combine vocabulary from two (or possibly three) topics to answer a Task. For example, a Task may ask about the effect of economic problems on the countryside, and you would then use vocabulary from Topics 7 and 9.

Topic 7 example Task

'Unemployment remains the biggest challenge to school-leavers in most countries'

How far do you agree with this assessment? What other challenges face young people today?

(school-leavers = young people who leave school without going on to further studies.)

Explanation of the Task

This is another Opinion > Personal viewpoint type essay (it asks how far you agree with an idea.) You should introduce the topic and give your opinion in the introduction, then explain why you have this view. You should briefly consider the opposing view, then restate your opinion in the conclusion. This particular Task has an extra element, which sometimes happens in Task 2: it asks you to suggest some other challenges also. You should combine these ideas in the main body of the essay, as in the example below.

Band 9 model essay

Youth unemployment is certainly a worrying **challenge** for most countries, especially at a time of **economic instability** and **social unrest**. However, to say that this is the largest **issue** is to overlook a range of equally **pressing matters,** as we will discuss now.

It must be admitted that **joblessness** can undermine a young person's **economic prospects** and consequent **social mobility.** Nevertheless, this issue can be ameliorated by coordinated action between the state and the **private sector,** as we have seen, for instance, in Canada recently. When this is realized, we can see that other concerns are at least as serious.

Foremost among these is perhaps the issue of age **demographics**, whereby young people bear the burden for an increasingly elderly population with high **longevity**. This means that young people will pay higher taxes and work longer hours, possibly forcing them to **migrate** to countries where this pressure is lower. The effect of this is the **'brain drain'** situation which can be seen in southern Europe, where young, ambitious people prefer to leave their countries altogether, exacerbating the problem for those remaining.

Furthermore, we must remember that a substantial proportion of young people globally face **existential threats** such as **famine, drought** or **outbreaks** of disease. These problems are often caused by (or are compounded by) **civil war, political instability** or the **corruption** of people in power locally. Such risks are a danger to their safety in addition to their **livelihood**, and so would appear to be far more serious than unemployment.

To conclude, it seems logical to accept that joblessness is a major challenge for young people. However, persistent trends in demographics among **developed countries** and the presence of physical dangers in **developing countries** should be regarded as at least as severe.

(290 words)

<u>Explanation of the topic vocabulary and examples in speaking</u>

a challenge = a problem or difficulty to be faced.

The West faces many challenges due to its ageing population.

economic or political instability = a rapid, unmanaged change in a country's economy or political situation.

Economic instability causes many people to move abroad to seek reliable work.

social unrest = riots, protests or fighting by the public against each other or the government.

Social unrest is spreading from the countryside to the cities, and the police are not responding.

an issue = a topic, subject or question that must be considered.

The issue of petrol price inflation is not often discussed in the media.

pressing matters = urgent, important issues.

I could not go to the college reunion because of more pressing matters at home with my family.

joblessness = a synonym for 'unemployment.'

Joblessness among older people is actually higher than among recent graduates.

economic prospects = the future possibilities for a national economy.

The economic prospects for very small countries are quite positive these days.

social mobility = the ability of people to progress in terms of salary, lifestyle and social status.

The greatest aid to social mobility is good education and training.

the private sector = private businesses, as opposed to 'the public sector' meaning state-owned or controlled services.

I definitely want to work in the private sector after I graduate. It is a more stimulating environment than the public sector.

demographics = the changes in society in terms of age, income, numbers, origins and location in a country.

Demographic changes in Scandinavia have been dramatic, with substantial immigration and an ageing indigenous population.

longevity = the tendency to have a longer life expectancy.

Japanese people have perhaps the highest longevity in the world.

to migrate = to move permanently between countries.

Migration within the Eurozone is a highly controversial issue at present.

'brain drain' = the tendency for intelligent or successful workers to migrate out of a country.)

Southern Europe is experiencing a high 'brain drain' these days, because of the lack of economic prospects.

existential threats = a threat to existence or life.

The economy of my country faces an existential threat from collapsing oil revenues.

an outbreak = the start of a widespread problem such as disease or conflict.

The outbreak of Ebola is a great concern for doctors globally.

civil war = war between people inside a country.

It will take many years for our nation to recover from the civil war of the 1990s.

livelihood = the way a person makes a living.

Many villagers sell handicrafts, as this is the only livelihood they can find.

developed countries = countries considered to have advanced economies, industries and social infrastructure.

Developed countries contribute aid to those nations affected by famine.

developing countries = countries not generally considered to be fully developed yet.

Illiteracy is a huge challenge for developing countries to overcome.

Topic 8: Cities and Infrastructure

About Topic 8

The cities and infrastructure topic includes the organisation of urban transport, communications and housing, trends in city life, social problems associated with cities such as overcrowding and petty crime, the growth of cities, possible future developments in city living, and comparisons of urban and rural lifestyles.

This topic is often used for Task 2 Ideas > Problem/solution and Ideas > Cause/effect type essays. There is also sometimes a connection to **Topic 9 Countryside and Agriculture,** so you may need to combine vocabulary from the two topics.

Topic 8 example Task

Transport delays and long journey times are a widespread phenomenon in many cities today. What are the causes of this problem, and how could the situation be improved?

Explanation of the Task

This is an Ideas > Mixed > Causes/solutions type essay. It does not ask for your opinion, but wants you to suggest some ideas about the causes of a problem situation and also some possible solutions. You should introduce the topic, describe two or three causes, then two or three solutions, and then summarise.

Task 2 sometimes mixes Cause/effect and Problem/solution Tasks in this way. You should read the Task very carefully to see if it is a 'mixed' type. The word 'problem' does not *necessarily* mean it is a Problem/solution Task.

Band 9 model essay

Transport is an essential part of **urban** life, and lengthy journeys are frustrating and expensive for those concerned. There appear to be two main causes of this, and several possible solutions, as we will explain here.

Perhaps the main cause is the lack of **investment or funding for infrastructure** in the form of **high-capacity public transport** and increased road space for private vehicles. This means that too many vehicles use the existing network, and **congestion** is inevitable. We see this in most large cities globally, such as London or Tokyo. Many **conurbations** also lack finance for **transport hubs**, such as integrated road and rail **facilities** which could connect public and **private transport**, thus reducing **bottlenecks**. A further cause seems to be the problem of **overcrowding** in cities, whereby people migrate from the **hinterland** and **settle** in urban areas, putting strain on **amenities**, housing and above all on transport capacity. This means that an already stretched system is often pushed to a critical point, causing cancellations and breakdowns in the technology used, especially in situations of **urban sprawl** such as in Latin America.

Regarding potential solutions, probably the main remedy would be to encourage investment in better infrastructure, for example through subsidies or **public-private partnerships** as was tried successfully in Germany during the 1990's. This enhances the network and fosters a sense of **civic pride**, to everyone's benefit. Another solution may be to use **tax incentives** to allow more **home working**, so that there is less need to **commute** from the **suburbs** to the **inner city** for work. A final response might be the development of more flexible patterns of transport, such as **communal car-pooling**, which would reduce reliance on existing systems and vehicles.

In conclusion, it seems that **outdated** infrastructure and overcrowding are the key factors behind our transport frustrations. Possible solutions would involve better funding, and also **innovations** in ways of working and travelling to reduce the **burden** on the system.

(311 words)

Explanation of the topic vocabulary and examples in speaking

urban = adjective meaning 'about cities.'

Urban crime is a great concern for the authorities in most countries today.

investment or funding = money to pay for an activity, either from government or business.

My home town secured investment from a charity for a new stadium, and funding from a local company for sponsorship.

infrastructure = the physical and system organisation of a city, area or country, especially in terms of transport and communications.

The UK railway infrastructure dates back to the 1860's in many places.

high-capacity = able to handle high volumes of goods or people.

Sea container ships are high-capacity international freight providers.

public transport = transport such as buses and trains funded by the state (as opposed to 'private transport' such as cars owned by individuals.)

I usually get to work by public transport, even though it's very crowded.

congestion = situation of too much traffic, causing delays (the phrase 'traffic jam' is not generally used in Academic English.)

I have to leave home very early in the mornings, because of the congestion on the way to my college.

conurbations = very large cities which have absorbed other towns.

Sao Paolo is a huge conurbation in Brazil, and is still expanding.

transport hubs = centres where many routes converge.

Heathrow airport is the largest transport hub in Europe.

facilities and **amenities =** places providing any service to the public, either private or public sector.

My home city has many amenities such as swimming pools and parks, and several facilities for elderly people such as care homes.

a bottleneck = a place where congestion regularly happens.

The connection from a motorway to a local road is always a big bottleneck.

overcrowding = a situation where too many people try to live in one place.

Hong Kong has managed its overcrowding problem very skilfully.

hinterland = the area around a city affected by its development.

I live in the hinterland of our capital city, where we regularly go for shopping and for work projects.

to settle in a place = to move and live there permanently, usually with work and a family.

I was born in Asia, but my parents settled in the USA when I was very young.

urban sprawl = the situation where a city expands and buildings are constructed without control or laws.

Urban sprawl has resulted in the rapid expansion of many Asian cities, with resulting damage to the environment.

public-private partnerships = projects funded jointly by the government and business, to reduce the cost to the taxpayer.

My country has just installed a new tunnel under the central mountains, run by a public-private partnership.

civic pride = the pride felt in the town/city where you live, its people and infrastructure.

As a symbol of civic pride, we built a new park zone with sports amenities and educational exhibitions.

tax incentives = reductions in tax to encourage people to do or buy something.

We should use tax incentives to encourage more people to try using their own solar panels at home.

home working = working in your home for all or part of the week.

Home working can be quite an isolated way to do your job.

to commute = to travel a long distance to work every day.

I live in the suburbs and commute by train to the city centre.

suburbs = the residential areas around a city.

Life in the suburbs can be rather boring, to be honest.

the inner city = the older, central part of a city.

Inner city housing is often overcrowded and noisy.

communal car-pooling = a voluntary system for people to travel in a shared car, to reduce fuel use.

I tried car-pooling, but it was difficult to arrange the journeys with three other people.

outdated = old-fashioned and not relevant today.

I find that our political parties are very outdated these days.

innovations = new ideas or things (which are usually useful or exciting.)

Mobile computing was one of the great innovations of the last ten years.

a burden = a weight or responsibility which is difficult to cope with.

The burden of income tax is much too high these days for normal people.

Topic 9: Countryside and Agriculture

About topic 9

The countryside and agriculture topic covers social and physical changes in the countryside, rural versus urban lifestyles, ways of using the countryside, and methods of farming including animals and crops.

It may seem surprising, but agriculture is actually one of the most common topics in IELTS across the Writing, Reading, Speaking and Listening tests. This means that you should definitely learn to use agriculture vocabulary as part of your exam preparation, even if the subject is not personally interesting for you.

Topic 9 example Task

It is sometimes said that the countryside offers a high quality of life, especially for families. What are the arguments for and against families choosing to live and work in the countryside, for example as farmers? What is your own view about this?

Explanation of the Task

This is an Opinion>Discussion type Task. You should introduce the topic, present two or three ideas on each side of the discussion, and then give your opinion in the conclusion.

The Task asks you specifically to think of families and the example of farmers, so you should include some ideas about this. Always check carefully to see if the Task has any extra or specific instructions such as this – if you miss these, it may affect your score badly.

Band 9 model essay

There can be few choices in life more important than where to settle as a family, and the question of an urban or **rural** location is complex. There are strong arguments for and against living in the countryside, as we will discuss now.

On the one hand, it might be said that the countryside is rather a **backwater**, with fewer cultural amenities than a city in the form of museums, theatres and even sporting events. This may mean that families become isolated, especially as **rural depopulation** leaves fewer **country dwellers** in the area, as we see, for example, in central France. Added to this is the **scarcity** of schools and colleges, meaning that children may need to travel long distances for their education. Finally, career options may be more limited in the countryside for both parents and children, resulting in **rural unemployment** and long-term **rural poverty** in the worst cases.

Conversely, life in the countryside has rewards which go beyond **material considerations.** For example, the **abundance** of natural resources such as land, **wildlife forestry and water bodies** means that a comparatively simple life can be lived at a **subsistence** level. Many country residents are **self-sufficient smallholders** in this sense, safeguarding them from the changes in **the wider economy** which can **afflict city dwellers**. If the parents are farmers, children learn the importance of **animal husbandry**, methods of farming such as **crop rotation and** irrigation, and generally may become more in tune with the natural world as a result. Finally, as technology enables children to undertake distance learning or **remote viewing** of cultural attractions such as museums, they should be less isolated from their cultural heritage.

Overall, it seems to me that quality of life in the countryside today is indeed quite high, with its advantages of resources, self-sufficiency and **environmental awareness**. This is especially true now that communications are reducing the risk of isolation in such **far-flung** communities.

(317 words)

Explanation of the topic vocabulary and examples in speaking

rural = the adjective for 'countryside.'

I come from a rural area originally, although these days I live in our capital city.

a backwater = an area of a country where little of interest happens.

I used to live in an agricultural town, but frankly it was such a backwater that I moved to one of the larger cities.

rural depopulation = the long-term trend for people to migrate from the countryside to cities, leaving the rural areas with few people.

Rural depopulation can cause huge problems with local infrastructure, as there aren't enough people to run the services and transport.

country dwellers = people who live in the countryside ('city dwellers' = people who live in cities.)

My parents were country dwellers when they first married, but now we all live in a coastal town.

a scarcity = a lack or shortage of something.

The worst problem I experienced in the countryside was a real scarcity of sports events and music festivals.

rural unemployment = unemployment affecting rural workers specifically.

Rural unemployment has been ameliorated by innovative Internet start-ups.

rural poverty = being extremely poor in the countryside.

Rural poverty is a long-term situation exacerbated by lack of infrastructure and training.

material considerations = concerns about money and material possessions.

You can't only think of material considerations when deciding who to marry, I feel.

an abundance = a very high level of supply or availability of something.

In the mountains, there's an abundance of wild flowers and goats.

wildlife = animals living naturally in the wild.

It's surprising how much wildlife you can see in the suburbs in Australia.

forestry = the industry of growing and cutting trees.

When I graduate, I want to work for a responsible forestry company.

water bodies = inland areas of water (rivers, lakes, reservoirs etc.)

My country is very arid and has almost no water bodies.

subsistence = adjective meaning 'producing just enough to live on'

Subsistence farmers grow their own food but have little left to sell for profit.

self-sufficient = not needing to import or buy resources from outside the farm or country.

During the war, our country became self-sufficient in crops and fuel.

smallholders = farmers managing very small farms, usually with their families.

I worked on a project training smallholders in South America in how to lobby politicians for reform.

the wider economy = the national economy in a country.

My business is growing, despite the decline in the wider economy.

to afflict = to affect (used for problems or diseases.)

Many forests in my area are afflicted by wood disease which attacks the trees.

animal husbandry = the skill of keeping animals.

My sister studied animal husbandry at college and enjoyed it enormously.

crop rotation = the process of using different fields each year to keep the soil healthy.

Some smallholders do not practise crop rotation, and so their land becomes infertile.

remote viewing = viewing places by Internet, not in person.

I took a remote viewing tour of the Metropolitan Museum in New York, and found it very impressive.

environmental awareness = an understanding of environmental issues.

Environmental awareness is part of the school curriculum these days for most children.

far-flung = remote or far away.

My fiancé lives in a very far-flung village, but we keep in touch by Zoom.

Topic 10: Government and the Authorities

About Topic 10

The government and the authorities topic mostly includes law and order, crime and policing, justice and punishment. Occasionally the Task may refer to ways of managing public services, and relations between countries.

The Tasks may ask about public policy in terms of funding (E.g. 'How should prisons be run – by governments or by private organisations?') but will not ask for your political views or about actual events in specific countries.

Topic 10 example Task

Some observers say that police officers should be recruited from the communities where they work, so that they have local knowledge. Other people say that this is unnecessary, or even undesirable. Where do you stand on this debate? Is local knowledge essential in modern policing?

Explanation of the Task

This is an Opinion > Personal viewpoint Task. You should introduce the topic and give your opinion in the introduction, then explain why you have this view. You should briefly consider the opposing view, then restate your opinion in the conclusion. The Task has the specific instruction to decide if you think local knowledge is 'essential,' so you should refer to this as part of your opinion.

Band 9 model essay

The need for effective, **trustworthy** police officers is **paramount** in society today, especially as criminals become more **devious** and creative. Regarding whether police should be locally hired, there is a case to be made on both sides of the debate.

Those who support local recruitment of officers point to the need for the police to understand the **minutiae** of the local community. For example, a community may have certain **frictions** or a history of a specific **grievance**, whether religious, political or otherwise. In such situations, the argument goes, the police need to show **sensitivity**, and also be able to anticipate the kinds of crimes that may be **committed**. Furthermore, local officers may find it easier to gain **informants** in the community, leading to stronger **evidence** at **trials**, higher **conviction** rates and a **deterrent** to crime through **sentencing, imprisonment, fines** or **community service** leading to **rehabilitation** of the **offender**.

On the other hand, it seems likely that officers from the community may in fact share some of the **tendencies** of the people they grew up with. For example, in countries such as Mexico, we see a high incidence of **corruption** among the local business and government community which is equalled by **bribery** among the police. A second objection is that local sensitivity may lead to the police failing to **enforce laws** fully, and effectively making exceptions for some offenders, which is **unequitable** towards **law-abiding** citizens. Finally, we must remember that police officers should have **transferable skills**, such as **lateral thinking** and **investigative** ability, which should **transcend** their background or the environment they are working in.

Overall, it seems to me that local knowledge is not absolutely essential for the police, whose skills should be effective in any **context**. Indeed, I agree with those who say that the risks of local recruitment **outweigh** the benefits, because of the danger of corruption and **over-familiarity** with potential offenders.

(318 words)

Explanation of the topic vocabulary and examples in speaking

trustworthy = capable of being trusted.

In most countries, politicians are regarded as untrustworthy and possibly corrupt.

paramount = of the greatest importance.

It is paramount that we find a solution to the problem of Internet piracy.

devious = extremely clever in a dishonest way.

Online criminals today are devious, and use many different methods to deceive their victims.

minutiae (pronounced 'my-new-shy') = very small details.

Nobody really understands the minutiae of the new tax code.

grievance = an issue which makes people upset or angry for a long time.

Some towns in the countryside have a grievance with central government because of land reform laws.

sensitivity = being alert to the circumstances of a specific group of people.

Teachers should show sensitivity to students who have language difficulties.

to commit an offence/a crime = to do or carry out the offence.

The President committed murder when he arranged for his opponent to be assassinated.

informants = people who tell the police useful information about criminals in their area.

The police paid the informant for information about who organised the riots.

evidence = material presented in court to prove that someone is guilty or innocent.

The police had a lot of DNA evidence against her, but no witness statements.

a trial = the legal procedure of prosecuting someone for a crime.

A murder trial can last for many weeks and cost millions of dollars to conduct.

conviction rates = the percentage of accused people who are convicted of (= found to be guilty of) a crime.

Conviction rates for burglary are low; only about 30% of trials result in a conviction.

a deterrent = something that makes people *not* want to do something (verb = to deter.)

We have a guard dog as a deterrent against intruders at night. It deters people from coming into our garden.

sentencing = the action of telling a convicted criminal what the punishment is

(verb = to sentence.)

Imprisonment = punishment by being in prison.

He was sentenced to five years imprisonment for the armed robbery of a shop.

A fine = money paid as a punishment.

The fine for speeding in my country is about 200 Euros.

community service = punishment by doing manual work for the public.

Her community service consisted of cleaning the town parks and sweeping litter in the streets.

rehabilitation = the process of changing a criminal's character so that he does not commit more crimes (verb = to rehabilitate someone)

Some prisons use music and drama to rehabilitate offenders. Others say there is no point in trying.

an offender = a person who commits an offence.

The government should provide training for offenders in prison, so that they don't turn to crime again when they leave.

tendencies = inclinations due to your character (usually negative.)

Some young people in cities have tendencies towards graffiti and vandalism.

corruption = the crime when an official breaks laws to help people that he knows.

Corruption is widespread in the police in some developing countries.

bribery = the crime of giving money to officials to get something done (verb = to bribe someone.)

I had to bribe a customs inspector to get my luggage through the airport.

to enforce laws = to apply them to people.

The police are not enforcing the laws about dropping litter in public. They should arrest more people for this.

unequitable = unfair or different for different groups.

It is unequitable to arrest young people for speeding, but not older people.

law-abiding = following all the laws in a proper way.

I am a law-abiding citizen. I never break the speed limit or any other laws.

transferable skills = skills that can be used in different situations.

I have transferable skills which I use in both my professional career and my fund-raising work for charities.

lateral thinking = the ability to think creatively and in new ways.

Tik Tok and Google are examples of companies that have grown by lateral thinking.

investigative = adjective from 'to investigate' = to enquire about the causes of a crime or a problem.

The police refused to investigate the Prime Minister, leading to accusations of corruption.

to transcend a situation = to be bigger or go beyond it.

The need for reducing financial waste transcends the government – everybody should be spending money more carefully.

a context = a specific situation.

Armed police evidently work well in the American context, but would be less effective in a British context.

to outweigh = to be more important than.

The advantages of having an electric car outweigh the costs.

over-familiarity = when an official is too friendly with the public.

We should discourage over-familiarity between judges and lawyers, because it could lead to corruption.

Developing Your IELTS Vocabulary

That completes our explanation of the ten IELTS vocabulary topics. It's very important now to try to start using these words in your speaking and writing as much as possible.

In addition to reading this book, try to maintain an interest in the ten IELTS topics by reading articles, web posts and stories on these subjects in the media. This will let you see further examples of how these words and phrases are used, and may also show you some further vocabulary which you can use. Reading about the topics will also give you evidence, examples and statistics which you can include in your IELTS essays and spoken answers, showing the examiner that you are well-informed and able to use sources to support arguments.

Many successful IELTS candidates keep a vocabulary record split into the ten topics, and add new words they encounter as a way of building up even more vocabulary, with examples of how it is used in context. The more you can do this, the more natural and advanced your English will be in the writing and speaking tests.

BOOK THREE
25 Task 2 Model Essays

Book Three: 25 Task 2 Model Essays

Introduction to Book 3

As IELTS examiners and teachers, we often meet candidates whose English is good but who have great difficulty with IELTS Writing Task 2. These candidates are unaware of the different types of essays they may need to write, and often lack sufficient academic vocabulary to raise their score to the top bands which they need. If that seems like you, this book will help enormously.

This book will guide you to get the best possible result in your IELTS Task 2 writing test. We will show you twenty-five Band 9 model essays which cover the different possible types of tasks you can meet in the exam. Each essay has an explanation of the task, suggesting ways for you to plan and write the essay, and also some brilliant comments from IELTS examiners which explain why the essay is marked at Band 9. The examiner also selects from each essay some of the best examples of vocabulary for you to use in your future essays.

By using this book and following its advice, you should improve your current band greatly and get the result you deserve.

Jessica Alperne & Peter Swires
Cambridge IELTS Consultants

cambridgeielts@outlook.com

Section 1: Discussion Type Essays

Essay 1 (Topic: Healthcare, Health & Sport)

Example Task

You should spend about 40 minutes on this question.

International sports events are sometimes said to be a good way of building understanding between countries; other people feel they serve little purpose, considering the cost. Discuss both aspects and give your own view.

You should give reasons for your answer, and include ideas and examples from your own knowledge and experience.
Write at least 250 words.

Explanation of the Task

The discussion type task is the most common type in Task 2. This type asks you to debate both sides of an issue and then give your own opinion. The best way to structure these essays is the classic layout of: a short introduction which does not give your opinion, then two large main paragraphs giving each side of the debate, and then a short conclusion giving your opinion. It is best if the side of the debate presented in the second main paragraph is the side which you support, because this will link smoothly to the conclusion:

Introduction giving context and background to the topic

Main Paragraph supporting side A

Main paragraph supporting side B

Conclusion giving your opinion, which supports side B

The task will usually include some key concepts to guide the debate; here, the key words are 'building understanding' and 'the cost,' so the essay should discuss these themes.
You essay will be more convincing and easier to follow if you can connect at least some of the points made in the second main paragraph with those made in the

first main paragraph; this shows that you have considered both sides fully. This method is used in the following essay, about international sporting events.
(All the essays in this book use American spelling. In the IELTS exam, it does not matter whether you use American or British English, but try to use one or the other consistently through your writing - try not to mix them.)

Band 9 Model Essay

Sporting events demand substantial resources, especially at international level, and people understandably wonder what benefit they bring. Arguments can be made to oppose or justify such occasions, as we will see.

Critics of these events cite the huge expenditure which they require, saying that the funds often come from taxpayers' money, and that the resources should be used instead to address urgent social problems within the country. For example, when Brazil hosted the football world cup, mass demonstrations erupted demanding that the money be diverted to jobless and environmental relief programs. Another objection to such events is that they actually increase tensions between countries, as rival supporters clash with each other. Finally, there is an environmental objection, as the amount of fuel and energy needed to organize a major event is considerable.

In answer to this, enthusiasts for international sports point out that these events are often largely self-funding, using advertising and sponsorship rather than public money. For example, international motor racing uses no state funding at all, and brings together huge numbers of people from different countries with no tension or hostility. Even when events are publicly funded, such as the Olympics, the building of new infrastructure and the spike in employment is itself of great benefit to the population, even after the games close. Few people would dispute that such events broadly increase goodwill between nations, despite occasional disputes and outbreaks of disorder. Admittedly, the environmental criticism is a challenge that still needs to be met, with a more careful use of energy by competitors and spectators.

To sum up, I feel that such occasions generally have a clear benefit in terms of use of both funds and international relations, provided that their environmental impact is properly managed.

(289 words)

Examiner's Comments

This is a very persuasive and well-organized essay, which gets Band 9 for its answering of the task and its use of academic English.

The introduction gives some background and makes it clear that this is going to be a discussion essay, leading the reader into a discussion of both sides. The first main paragraph makes three points against sports events (the points are: funding, tension and environment) and the example of Brazil is a good illustration of one of these points. The second main paragraph takes each of those three points in turn and argues against two of them, while conceding that the third one (environment) has some merit.

This allows the writer to give a balanced conclusion. This means the conclusion supports one side of the debate but also includes a condition; in this case, the condition is that we need better environmental management. Adding balance or nuance to the conclusion is a good way of raising the essay's likely band score.

This essay has some excellent language for describing the way that issues are debated by the authorities and within society. For example,

Critics cite (+ evidence) (to cite evidence = to state it as part of making an argument)
To address problems
To erupt (= to start suddenly and explosively)
Self-funding
A spike (= a surge or peak)
Outbreaks of disorder
Properly managed

The use of examples and evidence throughout is very strong: Brazil, motor racing and the Olympics are very relevant without being complicated.

Essay 2 (Topic: Education & Schooling)

Example Task

Some people feel that human history is an important field of study, while others say that the past has little relevance to today's world. Discuss both sides of this discussion and give your opinion.

Explanation of the task.

This is another typical discussion type task, asking for a consideration of both sides and an opinion. A key word in this task is 'relevance,' and the essay should consider this concept in the discussion. The focus is also on human history as a 'field of study,' implying that we are debating the study of history at an advanced level and discussing whether this is 'important' today.

This is a potentially controversial topic, and the essay needs to avoid being emotional or too one-sided, whatever the views of the person writing it.

Band 9 Model Essay

The question of whether it is relevant to study historical events, and how to use such analysis, is an interesting one in its own right.

People who discount the importance of historical study often highlight the huge differences between the past and today. In this worldview, the lives of people from centuries or millennia ago are somewhat irrelevant to today's life with its modern concerns. This perspective suggests that the resources currently devoted to history would be better used solving today's challenges in society and technology. Some on this side of the debate also make the point that, by analyzing history, we may adopt the mistakes of the past. For example, they say, modern dictators often use theories about history to justify their actions.

This is surely a minority view, however, and most of us would probably welcome a role for historical studies in society. This pro-history perspective points out that, despite the contrasts between today and the past, human psychology remains constant, and people from even the distant past had similar hopes and anxieties to us. It is possible that by studying, for example, the conflicts which ravaged Europe historically, we might prevent such catastrophes recurring. Examples of this include the postwar reconstruction of Germany or the peace process in Northern Ireland. This makes history invaluable, and justifies the resources spent. It also answers the rather negative idea that studying the past may make us repeat its errors, because of course we also learn from the successes and innovations of our ancestors.

Overall, I feel that history is of great benefit to society, and that discouraging its study would actually be dangerous. By ignoring the painful lessons of the past, we risk a repeat of previous disasters without learning the means to cope with them.

(296 words)

Examiner's Comments

This Band 9 level essay answers the task fully with a very advanced use of academic style and language.

The introduction highlights the key task concept of 'relevant' which is then debated in the two main paragraphs. The first main paragraph makes a case against the relevance of history, using a sequence of three points. The second paragraph begins by implying the candidate's opinion ('surely a minority view, and most of us would welcome . . .') and goes on to answer the three points made in the preceding paragraph. This connection between the points in the two main paragraphs makes the debate very logical and clear to follow. The examples given (Germany and Northern Ireland) are appropriate, although no detail is given. The conclusion gives a clear and strong opinion without using any emotion.

The writer uses varied and convincing language to refer to points of view (e.g. worldview, perspective, this side of the debate, minority view.) The writer uses tentative language to put forward arguments (e.g. 'we may adopt . . . we might prevent . . . it is possible that') and this is typical of high quality academic writing. There is also some very strong vocabulary here to describe the debate taking place:

The resources currently devoted to history (devoted to = allocated to, in a financial sense)
Adopt the mistakes of the past
Justify their actions
A role for historical studies
Conflicts which ravaged Europe (to ravage something = to attack and destroy it violently)
It also answers the rather negative idea
The painful lessons of the past

I was especially impressed that the candidate's opinion was so clear but not expressed in a dramatic or overheated way, which is sometimes a problem even with an essay at the upper levels of band scores.

Essay 3 (Topic: Culture, Art & Traditions)

Example Task

It might be said that a country's traditional festivals should be preserved carefully so that they do not change. On the other hand, some people welcome these festivals changing and evolving over time. Discuss both views and give your opinion.

Explanation of the Task

This discussion type essay has the key concept of festivals being 'preserved' compared to being allowed to 'evolve.'

It is important with a topic like this not to describe too much detail or to write too much about your personal experience of these events. Remember, the instruction after every task to 'include ideas and examples from your own knowledge and experience' does *not* mean giving stories and details about your personal life; it means using things you know about in wider society generally, especially things you have learned from the news or the media.

Band 9 Model Essay

Festivals and the traditions that accompany them often embody important elements of a country's culture and heritage. The debate over whether to preserve them permanently has arguments on both sides.

On the one hand, people who want these events to stay the same say that they are a link to the past, especially to important events in a country's history. The French Bastille Day or Mexican National Day are examples of this, and both have a massive following. In this view, such festivals give a common sense of origins and purpose, and thus have a unifying effect on society at a time when it may be fracturing. Allowing these events to change, it is said, would rob them of their fundamental ethos and the social benefits they bring.

Conversely, people who favour the natural evolution of festivals say that these occasions can sometimes be so rooted in the distant past that they have little relevance today. For example, the British Guy Fawkes Night celebration has been preserved as a ritual while, paradoxically, few people now understand its original significance. It can also be said that what we regard as traditional festivals are often themselves evolutions of older events, and that such things are constantly changing as a natural process. This begs the question of who exactly would enforce the preservation of such events. For instance, if Americans start to celebrate Halloween or Thanksgiving in a new way, should their government somehow intervene? For most people, that would be an unthinkable intrusion.

Overall, I feel that we should allow festivals to adapt and change naturally as society changes. This means that some may indeed stay unchanged by popular demand, while others will evolve in order to stay relevant.

(287 words)

<u>Examiner's Comments</u>

This is a good instance of a Band 9 essay which combines highly effective use of examples and evidence with a clear discussion of the issues in the task. The English used is of a high academic standard.

The introduction makes a comment about the importance of the topic; it also highlights the key word 'preserve' and clarifies that this is a discussion type essay ('arguments on both sides.')

The first main body paragraph gives the pro-preservation argument, using phrases to report the view ('people say . . . in this view . . . it is said.') The examples of France and Mexico support the argument without being too detailed. The second main paragraph, in favor of evolution, again has evidence which is relevant and not excessive. The candidate uses a question ('should their government somehow intervene?') in a helpful way, and the answer supports the case.

The conclusion gives an opinion which links to the previous paragraph, and this responds to the 'change or evolve' requirement in the Task.

Some of the vocabulary here is notable for its sophistication:
To embody
To have a unifying effect
To fracture (= to break into pieces)
A fundamental ethos (ethos = spirit or essence of something)
Paradoxically (= in an apparently self-contradicting way)
To beg the question (= this makes us ask the question)
To intervene
An unthinkable intrusion (unthinkable = completely unacceptable)

Essay 4 (Topic: Government & the Authorities)

Example Task

Some countries have a system of compulsory military service for young people, while other countries do not see a need for this. Considering the arguments on either side, which system do you think is best for a country generally?

Explanation of the Task

This discussion type task includes an instruction to decide on the best system for a country in general terms. The essay will therefore need to consider military service from the perspective of society a whole.

This is another example of a task where you may be tempted to write a lot about personal events in your own life or about people you know, but this would not be relevant and would reduce the band score.

Band 9 Model Essay

Obligatory military service has huge implications for young people, and also for the military and wider society. The concept should be carefully evaluated before anyone is asked to make this commitment.

Supporters of compulsory service emphasize the sense of purpose which it can bring to young people, who are given tasks involving personal responsibility and problem-solving. This builds skills and experience which are invaluable throughout life, both at work and personally. A second argument in favor is the extra capacity which military service staff add to the armed forces; these staff can be used for tasks ranging from disaster relief to building infrastructure, as in Columbia or Switzerland, and not only for military duties. Finally, this type of service can reduce unemployment and prepare youngsters more fully for starting their careers.

On the other side, however, critics of the concept point out that, in reality, the work which conscripts do is usually quite menial and repetitive. They are also often treated harshly, which hardly equips them with any skills for their careers, and in many cases their military employers seem to be inventing tasks for them rather than utilizing their potential imaginatively. Indeed, countries such as Holland and Italy have now abandoned compulsory service, because the recruits have no useful part to play in a modern army. Admittedly, the idea of reducing unemployment is an attractive one, but this could probably be done more effectively through voluntary or charitable schemes.

In conclusion, I feel that compulsory service is a largely outdated practice which helps neither the conscripts, the military nor wider society. The intended benefits could be far better achieved through volunteer programs, which ideally would feed into civilian career paths.

(284 words)

Examiner's comments

This Band 9 essay achieves a great deal and has the ideal sort of word count for Task 2. The introduction puts the topic in context and picks up the key concept of 'society.' This introduction is very effective at paraphrasing from the task ('compulsory' becomes 'obligatory' and 'for a country generally' becomes 'wider society.') The first main paragraph has three points in support of 'compulsory service,' while the second main paragraph answers this with four points against. The conclusion makes the opinion clear and gives a justification for it ('benefits could be far better achieved through . . .')

There is good signposting of the stages of the essay in terms of sequence ('a second argument. . . finally . . . however . . . indeed . . . admittedly . . . in conclusion.') There is also some impressive language and some strong combinations of words (collocations):

Huge implications
To evaluate a concept (to evaluate something = to consider its value or benefits)
Sense of purpose
Invaluable skills
Menial work (menial = very basic and unskilled)
To equip someone with skills
To utilize potential
An outdated practice
Intended benefits
Career paths

Essay 5 (Topic: Education & Schooling/Work & Careers)

Example Task

Some people think that all young people should attend university if they possibly can. Others believe that programs such as apprenticeships are a much more positive pathway for the vast majority. Discuss both sides of this debate, and give your personal view.

Note: an apprenticeship is a non-university system where young people earn a salary while learning a workplace skill.

Explanation of the Task

This discussion type task asks about university compared to apprenticeships, in particular whether apprenticeships would be better for most people ('the vast majority.')

Occasionally, the task will give you a definition of a key word, as here, because its understanding is crucial to the essay.

Band 9 Model Essay

The massive expansion of universities in recent years means that, in some countries, almost all young people have this route as a possibility. There are arguments for and against this when compared to apprenticeship schemes.

On one side, those who support mass university attendance say that a degree allows young people to develop their full potential, both academically and personally. In this view, university attendance is in some ways an end in itself, presented as an enriching experience producing a well-rounded person. Another argument in support is that university helps students to build contacts and friends within their chosen career field, so that their entry to the workplace is effective. Finally, there is the higher earning potential of graduates throughout their careers, which hopefully generates a good quality of life for them and their families.

However, proponents of apprenticeships tend to be skeptical of the 'enriching' argument for degrees, saying that experience in a real workplace among colleagues is in fact a much better way to make someone a well-rounded personality. Apprenticeships also have the great advantage of enabling a person to earn a salary immediately, without accumulating high student debt. Certainly, if debt is weighed against salary potential, there often appears to be little difference between remuneration for graduates and well-qualified non-graduates. Lastly, apprenticeships often involve advanced qualifications and elements of study, meaning that successful apprentices are no longer the basic manual workers they once were.

Overall, I feel that for a majority of people an apprenticeship is a better option than university, with the advantages of immediate experience and salary. The sophisticated nature of many such schemes means that they should be considered as a first option in many cases.

(283 words)

Examiner's Comments

This Band 9 discussion type essay is organized in a classic way, with a neutral introduction and the opinion given in the conclusion. The main paragraphs have three points in each, two of which are connected between the two paragraphs (the points about 'enriching' and 'earning potential' are made and then countered.) This connection makes the essay coherent and persuasive. The conclusion is careful to answer the point about the 'majority' of people and gives reasons for the opinion which refer back to the main body.

It is noticeable that most of the sentences in the essay are complex, meaning that they contain two or more ideas, not just one. The writer uses a variety of ways to connect the ideas within the sentences, for example (the connecting phrases are underlined):

. . . an end in itself, presented as an enriching experience . . .

. . . within their chosen career field, so that . . .

. . . throughout their careers, which hopefully generates . . .

. . . the 'enriching' argument for degrees, saying that . . .

. . . elements of study, meaning that . . .

A candidate needs to use sentences of this complexity in order to achieve a Band 9 score.

Essay 6 (Topic: Nature, the Environment & Energy)

Example Task

Some people have suggested restricting the journeys which an aircraft can make each year, for example with a legal limit on the number of flights or the kilometers travelled. Consider the arguments for and against this idea, and reach your own conclusion.

Explanation of the Task

This discussion type task includes two examples of how the proposed measure might be enforced ('a legal limit on flights or kilometers.') However, the instruction is to discuss for and against the measure itself, and not to choose between these two options.

In many discussion type essays, the writer will make a connection between the points in the two main body paragraphs, meaning that some of the points in the second main paragraph will answer points made in the first. In the following model essay, the candidate makes three points in each paragraph, but you will see that he does *not* connect the points, and the essay is still highly effective. In the exam, you should spend about five minutes planning your essay, especially the main paragraph points. If you cannot think of a way to connect the paragraphs in these five minutes, just use the ideas that you have. It is essential to leave thirty minutes for writing the essay and another five minutes at the end for reading and checking it through.

Band 9 Model Essay

Aircraft undoubtedly contribute greatly to carbon emissions, and any attempt to reduce this should be welcomed. The introduction of an 'aircraft travel cap' might be effective, but there are also reasons to oppose it.

On the one hand, such a cap system would certainly have the immediate effect of reducing air pollutants by limiting the number of aircraft flying. This effect was observed, for example, as a by-product of the Covid emergency when air travel was reduced massively and atmospheric pollution was measurably lower. The cap would also reduce noise pollution, and have the added benefit of reducing visitors to vulnerable places where tourism is causing damage. Finally, the cap would encourage the development of more sustainable forms of travel, for example by sea or by non-polluting high-speed trains and vehicles.

However, there are several major drawbacks to the proposal. Firstly, the upheaval caused to international supply chains would be enormous, potentially jeopardizing food and medical supplies if imports and exports were curtailed. Secondly, many human passenger journeys are essential for family or business reasons, and a ban would be seen as unreasonable if someone needs to fly to visit a dying relative, for instance, or to rescue a firm employing thousands. Finally, we have to ask whether airlines could actually continue to operate under such circumstances, and indeed whether aircraft could be manufactured at all if their use was rationed once sold.

Overall, I feel that the disruption caused by such a cap would have profoundly damaging repercussions, and would probably provoke a backlash against environmental measures. It would be more logical to urgently develop non-polluting forms of transport, including the electric aircraft now in planning, as a viable alternative.

(281 words)

<u>Examiner's Comments</u>

This Band 9 essay contains a series of relevant and well-presented points which discuss the proposed legislation fully. The introduction has a sentence putting the essay in context, and then a second sentence demonstrating that the two sides are going to be debated.

The first main paragraph presents its points using linking phrases ('On the one hand . . . for example . . . also . . . have the added benefit of . . . finally') which guide the reader through this side of the argument. Although these points are not directly answered in the second main paragraph, this second paragraph has logical ideas and evidence which again are carefully introduced ('However . . . firstly . . . secondly . . . finally . . . indeed.') The opinion given in the conclusion links back to the arguments in the second main paragraph, in the classic way.

The writer uses 'would' throughout to show that we are discussing hypothetical outcomes of a policy that is being considered, but not a real situation (for which 'will' is more suitable.)

There is some advanced English in the essay which an examiner will notice:

Should be welcomed
A by-product of (= a product as a result of a separate process)
Measurably lower
Have the added benefit of
Major drawbacks
Supply chains

Potentially jeopardizing (to jeopardize something = to threaten or present a risk to it)

Curtailed (to curtail something = to shorten or limit it)

Profoundly damaging repercussions

Provoke a backlash against (a backlash = a violent negative reaction)

A viable alternative (viable = workable in reality)

Essay 7 (Topic: Education & Schooling)

Example Task

Many schools require pupils to wear a school uniform, while others allow children to wear any clothes they wish. What are the arguments for and against school uniform? Which option do you support?

Explanation of the Task

This Task asks for a straightforward discussion type essay with you supporting one of the sides. You could write this essay by organizing your four paragraphs in the classic pattern as:

Introduction

Paragraph supporting side A

Paragraph supporting side B

Conclusion with opinion supporting side B

Alternatively, a slightly different pattern is:

Introduction

Paragraph opposing side A

Paragraph supporting side A

Conclusion with opinion supporting side A

In this layout, you are considering both sides by discussing the arguments for and against only side A in the two main paragraphs. This does not mean you are neglecting side B, because the essay is still discussing both aspects; this is just an alternative structure for you to consider using if you wish. The model essay below follows this alternative structure.

Band 9 Model Essay

School is such a vital part of children's lives that any major change to its mandates needs to be carefully considered. The topic of school uniform can be quite controversial, with strong feelings for and against it.

Those who oppose school uniform often say, primarily, that standardized clothing suppresses a child's personality and imposes an artificial conformity on them. This view says that children should be as relaxed and comfortable as possible at school, and clothes are a key part of this. Another factor against uniforms is that many children wish to wear clothing associated with their original culture, which may be very different from the school requirement.

On the other hand, school uniforms exist for good reasons, and it may be unwise to challenge this long-standing logic. For one thing, uniforms prevent one child appearing richer or poorer than the next child, and so standard clothing helps prevent prejudice and hostility due to a family's income. Frankly, this argument seems hard to refute, when we consider the huge disparity in purchasing power between children's families even within the same classroom. Uniforms also guard against the danger of pupils becoming fixated on the fashion status of their leisure clothes, and demanding the latest items to compete with their peers. These are not theoretical dangers, but real problems which have arisen when uniforms have been abolished, as has been trialled in some American states, for example.

To sum up the debate, I strongly favor the retention of school uniform and the resulting standardization among young students. I feel that this prevents prejudice and friction which would otherwise occur, no matter how well-intentioned a more relaxed policy might be.

(277 words)

Examiner's Comments

This essay answers the task fully by debating the arguments against and then in favour of uniforms. This effectively also covers the argument for and against students wearing any clothes they wish, because that is the only alternative we are considering to uniforms. This structure works well with such an uncomplicated task.

The introduction emphasizes the importance of the subject and sets the scene for a discussion type essay. The first large paragraph reports the views of opponents ('Those who oppose . . . this view says . . . Another factor against uniforms . . .') using three ideas, which is the most suitable number for a main paragraph in Task 2.

The second main paragraph begins to clarify that the writer supports uniforms; this is done in a subtle way by saying 'it may be unwise to challenge (them) . . . this argument seems hard to refute . . . These are not theoretical dangers . . .' I would not normally expect the opinion to be expressed at this stage, but this is done carefully and indirectly. The conclusion confirms that the writer is strongly in favor, while still conceding that the opposing view has some merit ('no matter how well-intentioned . . .') This stops the essay being too one-sided and shows that the writer has considered both sides openly.

Impressive vocabulary used here includes a number of phrases which are suitable for Task 2 essays on any topic:

A mandate (= a legal order or instruction)
Conformity
To refute an argument (= to reject it and prove it wrong)
Disparity (= an unequal difference or gap)
Peers (= people at the same stage and level as you)
Retention, to retain (= to keep, maintain)
No matter how

Essay 8 (Topic: Education and Schooling)

Example Task

Some people believe that children should be taught foreign languages as soon as they start school, while others think that this should be left until later or even be completely optional. Consider the different aspects of this debate and give your own view.

Explanation of the Task

You may encounter this slightly different kind of discussion type task; it actually asks the candidate to consider *three* possibilities (early teaching of languages, later teaching or no compulsory teaching at all.) The essay will need to discuss the three options before giving the writer's own view. This means that the writer will need to decide carefully in what sequence to discuss the three possibilities, to keep the structure clear. The opinion should still be kept for the conclusion paragraph.

Band 9 Model Essay

The question of foreign language learning for children has always been rather controversial, and one's view is perhaps a cultural matter as much as an educational one.

Those who suggest starting the teaching at later stages point to the need to avoid overloading children academically at a very young age. This view says that lessons majoring on grammar or rote learning might be excessive alongside the existing demands of math, science and literacy. I feel that this perspective tends to overlook the potential for teaching languages in a non-academic way.

A further option is to remove the compulsory element and make foreign languages entirely optional. This view places language learning among the specialized subjects which children may not wish to pursue at all, allowing them to set their own fields of study which will hopefully make them more dedicated learners. This view, however, neglects the benefits which foreign languages could bring, outside of purely academic considerations.

Finally, proponents of compulsory language lessons in early years education say that children are most receptive at this stage, and so the teaching is more effective. There is also the potential benefit of exposing children to foreign cultures at an early age, to broaden their horizons culturally and encourage an interest in the wider world. Such teaching should not be rigorously academic or too demanding, however, but more of an exciting and involving lesson with the focus on enjoyment.

Overall, I would favor making languages compulsory at the earliest possible age, because of the great opportunity to expand children's global understanding through these lessons. I believe this would have the greatest benefit, even if the pupils do not go on to study the language academically.

(281 words)

Examiner's comments

At 280 words, this essay is the ideal length for Task 2, and would certainly achieve Band 9. It is very clearly structured, with an introduction raising the theme of 'culture vs education' which is then developed in the body and the conclusion. Each of the three main paragraphs connects clearly to one of the three options described in the task (compulsory teaching in early years, compulsory at later stages or completely optional.)

In each main paragraph, one or two points supporting each option are considered, along with a rebuttal in the case of paragraphs 2 and 3 (a rebuttal is a statement opposing the view just given, for example 'this perspective tends to overlook. . .' in paragraph 2 and 'This view, however, neglects . . .' in paragraph 3.) This gives the impression of a carefully balanced discussion.

Paragraph 4 gives a condition to the view supporting early years teaching which connects to one of the arguments given earlier ('not rigorously academic' connects with the earlier point of 'avoid overloading children academically.')

It is worth noting that the classic way to organize a normal discussion type essay is:

Introduction

Paragraph supporting option A

Paragraph supporting option B

Conclusion with opinion supporting option B

However, in this particular essay, the candidate is dealing with three options to debate, and so the structure is:

Introduction

Paragraph supporting option A with rebuttal

Paragraph supporting option B with rebuttal

Paragraph supporting option C

Conclusion with opinion supporting option C

It works well in this case, because the paragraphs supporting options A and B contain rebuttals which prepare the reader for the conclusion. The paragraph supporting C links to the conclusion supporting C which follows next.

The English used is academic and sophisticated. For example, the writer uses tentative language ('perhaps' 'potential' 'might be excessive') and also uses a variety of ways to report other opinions ('Those who suggest . . . point to . . . . . . this view . . . Proponents of . . .')

The writer has an excellent grasp of vocabulary and collocations on this topic (children's education), using phrases such as:

Early years education
Broaden their horizons
Rote learning (rote = a constant repetition to memorize something)
Compulsory syllabus
Specialized subjects
Fields of study
Academic considerations

Essay 9 (Topic: Education and Schooling)

Example Task

One view of education is that exams are the best measure of a young person's abilities, while another view holds that students should be continuously assessed by their teachers and given grades without taking exams. Discuss these views and give your own opinion.

Explanation of the task

This is a straightforward discussion type task which asks for a debate about two different views. The model essay below shows a different way of organizing these discussion type essays, which is:

Introduction

Paragraph supporting view A

Paragraph against view A and supporting view B

Conclusion supporting a combination of view A and B (a 'balanced conclusion')

You can use this structure for any discussion type essay, but make sure you can write discussion essays in the classic structure as well (the structure shown, for example, in essays 1 and 2 in this book.)

Band 9 Model Essay

The question of how to assess students most effectively is an important and complex one, with valid arguments for and against continuous assessment. We will consider these aspects and reach a conclusion.

Supporters of continuous assessment often point out the potentially unfair nature of exams, meaning that, if a pupil is ill or distracted on the day, their grade suffers despite their abilities. This can have severe implications for the young person's further studies or career, due to circumstances they cannot control. Another factor against testing is that many other students who are strong in their subject simply do not perform well under exam conditions, meaning that their potential is undermined regardless of their expertise. Finally, there is always the possibility of cheating in exams, leading to a person falsely presenting themselves as qualified; in areas such as medicine, this can be highly dangerous.

On the other hand, continuous assessment is far from an ideal solution. The assessment process inevitably uses up considerable teaching time, meaning that the subject itself may be neglected. Furthermore, the question of the relationship between the assessing teacher and the student is controversial; many of us have witnessed cases where pupils are over or under graded due to apparent favoritism or hostility from the teacher. Some people would also say that this human element is also open to corruption, creating the same danger as cheating in exams. Lastly, it is widely recognized that exams give students a clear milestone to work towards, creating a purpose and focus in their studies which continuous assessment may lack.

Overall, I would beware committing exclusively to either exams or assessment. In a modern curriculum, it should be possible to combine the best features of both to produce a fair and effective testing regime which is both accurate and unbiased.

(300 words)

Examiner's Comments

300 words is quite a long essay, but the writer has used very clear organization to make the essay easy to read. It does not follow the classic discussion type layout, but nevertheless the structure answers the task fully by evaluating assessment versus exams and giving an opinion. The opinion itself is balanced (a combination of both views) and this is an element typical of good quality academic English.

I noticed that the writer uses an example of behavior which she seems to have personally witnessed ('apparent favoritism or hostility from the teacher.') Normally, personal testimony like this does not work well in Task 2; however, this is introduced as a general example (she writes 'many of us have witnessed cases' and not something such as 'I myself have witnessed a case') and so this is still a relevant and effective point to make.

The candidate uses good linking words to guide the reader ('Another factor . . . finally . . . On the other hand . . . furthermore . . . lastly.') There are several collocations of a high standard ('severe implications . . . highly dangerous . . . ideal solution . . . human element . . . widely recognized.')

This essay would achieve Band 9 for Task 2.

Essay 10 (Topic: Culture, Art & traditions/Government & the Authorities)

Example Task

Some people think that, in the age of digital books and media, traditional public libraries have no further use. Others believe that public libraries will always have an important function. Considering both sides of this debate, how do you think public libraries can stay popular and relevant?
Note: a public library is a facility which lends books free of charge to the public.

Explanation of the Task

This is a more complex discussion type task; it asks for a discussion of whether or not libraries have a function today because of digital media, and also asks for suggestions on how they can stay relevant. The essay will need to combine the discussion with the suggestions in the main body, and give an opinion in the conclusion.

Band 9 Model Answer

Public libraries represent a substantial investment of space and resources, and the expense needs to be justified at a time when any mobile phone can have its own library of books and files.

It is understandable that some people believe our libraries are now largely redundant. There has been a massive shift from paper books to digital books, and the demand for physical borrowing has declined accordingly. This has been accelerated by the growth of innovative digital libraries from retailers such as Amazon, where a wide range of Ebooks can be borrowed for a small subscription. There is also a general decline in the reading of books as entertainment, as books now compete with podcasts and streaming events for the public's attention. It certainly seems possible that, if they do not adapt, traditional libraries will eventually become deserted.

On the other hand, this question of adaptation is crucial to their survival. For example, libraries could compete with online retailers to offer digital book lending subscriptions alongside their physical lending. They could also offer a delivery service to avoid the need for members to travel into town centers to borrow and return books. Furthermore, libraries could begin to provide a wider range of services which capitalize on their large physical space, for example by offering study areas, office facilities or even classrooms for private tuition. Lastly, they could seek to revitalize interest in paper books by involving the public more fully, for instance by hosting book festivals or other events to bring people in and compete with digital entertainment.

Overall, libraries are in a challenging era which will require some creative adaptation to stay relevant. By offering more imaginative facilities, and by cultivating greater public interest in traditional books, they can probably ensure that demand for their service continues.

(298 words)

Examiner's Comments

The candidate has organized this very clearly, considering that it could be a rather confusing essay with its combination of discussion and ideas. The introduction gives a context to the debate, which is the contrast between the traditional and the digital, without repeating vocabulary from the task.

The first main body paragraph gives reasons why libraries may not be relevant, and then the second main paragraph introduces the idea of 'adaptation' and gives the suggestions required by the task. The opinion is clear in the conclusion which also summarizes the discussion.

The number of points made in each main body paragraph seems appropriate, and all the information and examples are completely relevant.

The writer uses some impressive language to discuss trends ('a massive shift . . . has declined accordingly . . . accelerated') and also to describe innovations and improvements ('revitalize interest . . . capitalize on . . . involving the public . . . hosting festivals . . . cultivating interest.')

As an examiner, I notice that most of the sentences here are complex sentences, meaning that they include at least two elements or ideas; at the same time, the sentences are not over long, and they connect and follow on from each other logically. I would certainly give this essay a Band 9 score for its excellent organization, language and content.

Conclusion to Section One

This concludes our section on the discussion type essay. You have read ten Band 9 model essays showing the best ways to answer these tasks, plus a large amount of useful, advanced vocabulary which you can use in your own essays. Remember: it is essential to practice the discussion type essays a lot, because they are the most common in IELTS Task 2. The second most frequent type is the personal viewpoint type of essay, which is the subject of the next section.

Section 2: Personal Viewpoint Type Essays

Essay 11 (Topic: Global Challenges)

Example Task

'Carbon fuel vehicles should be eliminated without any further delay.'

How far would you agree with a proposal for a ban on petrol and diesel engines for road vehicles, with immediate effect?

Explanation of the Task

A personal viewpoint type task starts with a statement or a proposal about a situation. The instruction is then for you to say how much you agree or disagree with the statement. This might be expressed as *'To what extent do you agree or disagree'* or alternatively *'How far do you agree/support/approve of'* or a combination of similar phrases.

The classic way to organize your essay in answer these Tasks is:

Introduction which gives your opinion.

A large main paragraph, explaining and justifying your opinion.

A smaller main paragraph (the 'concession' paragraph) conceding some merit in the opposing view, but rejecting it.

Conclusion which summarizes and restates your opinion.

As you see, there is obviously a big difference between this type and the discussion type from essays 1 to 10 (where you express your opinion only in the conclusion.) The following essay uses this classic personal viewpoint pattern to answer the task above, about carbon fuel vehicles.

Band 9 Model Essay

Carbon fuel emissions continue to cause universal concern, and an immediate prohibition on such engines might seem an attractive solution. However, I feel this step would cause such disruption that it should not be implemented at present, for several reasons.

Firstly, we have to consider the purpose of such a ban. If the intention is to reduce global emissions, the ban would logically need to be enforced worldwide to achieve this goal. It seems highly unlikely that every country on earth would participate in this process; rather, we would see a mix of countries with bans, some with partial bans and many without. The reason for this uneven response demonstrates the second flaw in the proposal, which is that there is currently no exact replacement for the internal combustion engine for road use. While great strides have been made in electric vehicles, the cost of these transports and the infrastructure needed to recharge them mean that they are not a direct replacement. Attempting to enforce them now would massively disrupt global supply chains and travel, to the extent of endangering not only our lifestyles but potentially many lives as well. This upheaval would itself cause a backlash against electric vehicles, which would be counterproductive.

Of course, I accept the need to replace carbon fuel engines as soon as possible, but this should be part of a planned and phased process which uses electric vehicles as they evolve and become more versatile. This would safeguard the transport system and also ensure public support.

In summary, a ban should be part of our future goals alongside the urgent development of alternative vehicles. However, an immediate prohibition would probably risk undermining the very objective we are trying to achieve.

(286 words)

Examiner's Comments

This Band 9 essay is clearly organized and uses a high level of academic English, while answering the task completely. The word count is optimal for Task 2.

The introduction puts the statement in context and then gives an opinion on it. The large second paragraph then explains the writer's reasons, giving two points as evidence which are each discussed and explained effectively. There is then a shorter paragraph which contains a concession to the other point of view, agreeing with the broader intention of the proposal but commenting on the timing of it. This concession paragraph shows that the writer has considered the opposing view fully, and does not have a simplistic view. The conclusion briefly paraphrases and summarizes the opinion and the concession.

The candidate guides the reader through the essay with simple but effective linking words (e.g. 'However . . . firstly. . . of course . . . in summary.')

There are some very natural-sounding uses of vocabulary which confirm this is a band 9 level essay:

Universal concern

Partial ban
Uneven response
Great strides (= great progress)
Endangering our lifestyles
To undermine an objective (= to damage or weaken it)

Essay 12 (Topic: Government & the Authorities)

Example Task

'Stores should be prevented by law from offering price promotions on food products. The price should always be fair by law.'

To what extent do you agree with this statement?

Explanation of the Task

The key concepts in the task statement here are 'promotions prevented by law/price fair by law.' The task is not asking you to decide what kind of promotions should be offered on food, but whether this practice should be banned completely.

In the five minutes that you spend planning for Task 2 in the exam, if you have a personal viewpoint task, remember to include your idea for the small concession paragraph (which says that there is some merit or value somewhere in the opposing idea, although you still disagree with it and maintain your opinion.) This is a key feature of academic writing, because it prevents the essay being too one-sided. Remember, though, that the concession paragraph should be much smaller than the main paragraph which explains your opinion. For example, in the following essay about food promotions, the small concession paragraph and the conclusion admit that the law has a role to play, but this role is about regulation and not prohibition.

Band 9 Model Essay

The idea that the state should control food prices is becoming increasingly widespread in political circles. I feel that the proposal would be largely impractical in reality, despite its good intentions.

Firstly, we need to realise that food comes to stores through supply chains involving many stages and cost factors. It would be virtually impossible for governments to audit this process and decide what a 'fair' price is; indeed, the retail price is affected by factors outside the store's control such as shortages, gluts and seasonality. Furthermore, discounts and offers are an effective way of ensuring prices are broadly competitive, by allowing consumers to try products and decide for themselves if they are worth the cost of buying again. We should also be wary of allowing the state to interfere in markets within such a key sector of industry, because this may expand to other areas such as travel and even housing. The unhappy experience of citizens in the Soviet Union, for example, shows how unsuccessful a state can be at fixing the price of everything from food to rents and clothing.

At the same time, it is essential that the law does step in to protect consumers against misleading offers. Scandinavian countries, for example, have extensive legislation covering retail promotions, reassuring shoppers that they are not being manipulated by false offers.

Overall, I feel that the state's role should be to regulate promotions in consumers' interests, rather than establishing ongoing retail prices; these are best left to the markets.

(271 words)

Examiner's Comments

This essay, which is certainly graded at Band 9, responds to the task by giving a clear but qualified opinion (qualified means that the opinion includes a concession or condition showing that the debate is not completely polarized.) The introduction sets the ground for this by stating the candidate's opposition to the task statement while admitting it has good intentions.

The first main paragraph explains the reasons for the writer's opinion, which is expressed in a neutral way ('We need to realize . . . we should be wary of . . .') The concession paragraph links back to the task by saying that the law does have a function, but a qualified one. The conclusion is short, but it summarizes the opinion well.

The candidate uses a range of impressive language, for example in using adjectives and adverbs to describe events:

Increasingly widespread (= happening in many places)
Largely impractical
Virtually impossible
Broadly competitive (= generally, mostly)
Unhappy experience
Misleading offers
Extensive legislation
Ongoing prices

Essay 13 (Topic: Children & Families)

Example Task

'Social media can be a force for good, but is more often a cause of problems, especially for young people.' To what extent do you agree or disagree with this statement?

Explanation of the Task

The key concept in this statement is the balance between 'a force for good' and 'a cause of problems.' The essay will need to explain how far your personal viewpoint leans towards the 'good' or the 'problems' side, especially considering young people.

Remember, in IELTS task 2 you do not necessarily need to give your *real* personal opinion in the discussion or personal viewpoint essays. The examiner only wants to see that you can organize the essay and write it effectively, and there is no right or wrong assessment of the opinion itself. Many candidates therefore 'pretend' to have a certain opinion which is quicker and easier to present than their real opinion.

Band 9 Model Essay

Social media is so universal today that some problems will almost inevitably arise, above all for the young. I feel, however, that the advantages generally outweigh the dangers, with some caveats.

Social media can bring a number of benefits. It can, for example, allow young people to maintain a much wider and more varied circle of friends than used to be possible, and also to keep in contact with friends and acquaintances despite long distances. This makes people happier and more fulfilled, certainly compared to the days of phone calls and postage. Social media can also enable people to circulate factual information, such as advice on health or entertainment, which makes their peer group better informed. This is a major route for young people, especially, to gather and distribute useful advice. Finally, there is the great benefit of allowing young people to seek information on their studies and future careers, allowing them to make well-informed choices. It is also significant, of course, that all these benefits happen at much greater speed than would be possible without such applications.

Having said that, there is undoubtedly a danger for youngsters in being bullied or 'cancelled' by their peers on social media, especially in groups. However, these problems can hopefully be preempted and minimized by thoughtful education on best practice and considerate use.

In summary, I believe that the many benefits of social media, in terms of speed and breadth of sharing information, do ultimately outweigh the possible problems. This assumes that the potential for abuse is minimized, especially among the young who are the highest users.

(263 words)

Examiner's Comments

This Band 9 essay gives a balanced opinion in the introduction (social media is good but 'with some caveats') and then justifies the view effectively in the main paragraph. There are no specific examples given by the writer, but there are sufficient references to actual evidence (phone calls, postage, health, entertainment, careers) to make this persuasive. The next paragraph gives the 'caveat' which the reader is expecting, and explains why this problem is outweighed (the danger can be preempted.) Overall, this is an excellent example of a fairly short Task 2 essay which sets its outline in the introduction and then guides the reader through the delivery of that outline.

The writer uses some impressive vocabulary which candidates would find useful in essays on any topic:

To outweigh (= to be bigger or more important than something else)
A caveat (= a condition that you set while agreeing to something)
To circulate information
Well-informed choices
To preempt a problem (= to take action to prevent it starting)
Breadth (= width, the noun of 'broad')

Essay 14 (Topic: Nature, the Environment & Energy)

Example Task

'Policy to preserve nature and the environment should be the first priority for all governments.' To what extent do you agree with this suggestion?

Explanation of the Task

This task asks about where environmental policy should rank on a list of government priorities. It will therefore be possible for you to present a nuanced opinion (nuanced = containing subtle or complex differences in meaning; nuance = the noun.) For example, you might say that environment should be a joint first priority with other policies, or it should be first but with some caveats. This can often be included in the concession paragraph as part of conceding that the opposing idea has some merit.

Where possible, try to add nuance to your opinion, even in a brief way. This will usually involve setting conditions or caveats for your opinion, or making it dependent on certain factors.

Band 9 Model Essay

Governments need to embrace a range of policy goals, some of which overlap each other. Personally, I do not agree that the environment should be the first priority if that means neglecting other areas.

For example, economic policy is crucial to maintain a prosperous and stable society, which in turn produces tax revenue for the state. These revenues are key to enabling governments to pursue other policies, including environmental. This means that effective economic policies are actually the first step in preserving nature, rather than an unconnected process. The same can be said of education policy, which hopefully helps the population understand why environmental goals are important, and thus gains public support. A further area is international relations, through which governments can build relationships with other countries; these connections can then be used to achieve a variety of goals, among which the environment will certainly be a priority. In all these cases, we see that successful economics, education and diplomacy are the facilitators of further policies which a government may want to establish. The role of the government may then be to make the environment its main priority, once funding, public support and foreign relationships are in place.

This is not to say that policies in these three areas should themselves neglect their environmental impact. For example, Canada and Denmark have established economic programs which reflect environmental concerns over energy and land use, generating revenues which then feed into further nature initiatives. Hopefully, this process creates a virtuous circle which protects nature by 'joining up' all government activities.

In summary, we should be cautious of seeing the environment as a standalone priority for the state. Rather, it should be embedded in all policy areas, whose success then facilitates further environmental programs.

(291 words)

Examiner's Comments

This essay contains a lot of information and has quite a high word count, but its clear structure avoids any danger of it being confusing. The introduction gives a viewpoint which is evidently going to have some conditions attached to it. The large main paragraph builds up ideas by introducing the idea and then using 'this/these' to add explanation and evidence:

'For example, economic policy . . . these revenues . . . this means . . . A further area is international relations . . . these connections . . .'

This helps the writer present a large amount of material in a way that is clear to follow.

The concession paragraph explains the conditions which the candidate puts on the opinion (the virtuous circle process) and gives a relevant example without excessive detail. The conclusion is a clear summary of both main paragraphs.

It is well worth highlighting how the candidate uses verbs with nouns in a very natural way:

Ideas overlap each other
To pursue a policy
To gain support
To build relationships
To establish programs
To reflect concerns
To generate revenues

Also:

A facilitator/to facilitate (= something/someone that enables something to happen or develop)

To embed something in something else (= to make it part of the body or structure)
A standalone priority (= independent, unconnected to anything else)

Essay 15 (Topic: Culture, Art & Traditions)

Example Task

'Museums and art galleries should always offer free entry to visitors, enabling everyone to enjoy culture regardless of their income.' To what extent do you agree or disagree with this opinion?

Explanation of the Task

The statement in this classic personal viewpoint type task includes a point about visitor access to museums and galleries 'regardless of income.' The essay should therefore cover this element (of affordability) at some stage. When planning your essay in the exam, try to ensure you identify all the key concepts so that you answer the task as fully as possible.

Band 9 Model Essay

Cultural funding is a difficult issue, and perhaps one with no ideal solution. Personally, I do not believe that entry should always be completely free, and I will explain why.

Firstly, the cost of running such places as museums and galleries is quite high, considering the premises, contents and staff. This cost would not disappear if we offered free entry; rather, it would still be funded by the operator, which is often the state. This means that taxpayers would be paying for sites which might only have very few visitors, and in some cases would be largely deserted at off peak times. Imposing a small charge helps to offset this expense and ensures that there is at least some link between a venue's popularity and its income. This incentivizes the management to make the place more attractive to the widest possible audience, thus ensuring that more people do indeed benefit from its cultural offering.

Secondly, we should recognize that many sites are also privately operated, especially in the art world. Entry fees are an important revenue stream in this sector, and this income helps acquire more exhibits and to promote the work of aspiring or undiscovered artists. Forcing these galleries to open without charge would effectively oblige many of them to close, having the opposite effect to that intended.

This is not to say that we should not seek to encourage visits by people on limited incomes who might struggle to pay the full charge. A suitable compromise may be to publicly fund a discount scheme for students, the unemployed and pensioners, while other visitors pay the normal rate.

Overall, universal free entry would probably be counterproductive, and a charge, however low, should be retained visitors who can afford it.

(290 words)

<u>Examiner's Comments</u>

This Band 9 essay does a good job of reaching a balanced conclusion, in which the candidate makes it clear that she supports *part* of the statement idea but otherwise disagrees with it. The first main body paragraph contains a number of linked ideas (meaning ideas which build on the previous idea.) The writer uses 'this' to connect the concepts: 'This cost . . . This means . . . this expense . . . this incentivizes . . . thus ensuring . . .' This is a very effective method in a large paragraph such as this. The concession paragraph clarifies that the writer supports a compromise on entry charges which touches on the point about incomes. Suggesting a compromise or a 'half way house' is often an excellent way to make a concession and give a balanced or nuanced opinion. Finally, the conclusion is a brief summary of the debate and the opinion.

This is quite a long Task 2 essay, but the interconnected ideas and the use of language make it easy to read. The candidate uses an impressive range of vocabulary, especially to discuss funding and costs:

The premises (= the building where activity takes place)
To operate a site
Off peak times
To impose a charge
To offset an expense (to reduce it by using revenue from somewhere else)
To incentivize someone to do something (= to motivate them, usually with money)
Widest possible audience
A revenue stream
Aspiring (= hoping to do or become something)
To struggle to pay a charge
A suitable compromise
Counterproductive (= having a negative effect compared to the intention)

Essay 16 (Topic: The Countryside & Agriculture)

Example Task

It has been suggested that people should only eat food grown in their local area, and, where possible, people should also be involved in the farming of the food. How far would you agree with these proposals?

Explanation of the Task

This is an example of a task where the statement has more than one element for you to agree or disagree with (here, 'eat local' and 'be involved in farming.') You could decide to agree (or disagree) with both elements, or you could agree with one and disagree with the other. In this model essay, the writer disagrees with both the elements (local food + involvement in farming) but she supports the overall intention, producing a nuanced concession paragraph and a balanced conclusion.

Band 9 Model Essay

Achieving a healthy and affordable food supply is vital to a society, and any measure which helps attain this goal is welcome. I doubt, however, that the proposed ideas would be advisable, at least in their current form.

For one thing, we need to remember that not all the human population live in areas where food can be grown successfully. To say that people must eat local produce would be practical in North America or European coastal areas, for example, where a wide variety of food can be cultivated or caught. In arid or frozen climates, however, this would be unviable. Arab countries or those near the Arctic circle are examples of places relying on imports to feed their populations. As for the idea of residents working on the farms, this is an admirable concept if done on a voluntary basis with willing participants. If made compulsory, however, it becomes rather dystopian to most of us, and would surely be unenforceable without absolutely draconian measures which would be reminiscent of 1970s Cambodia.

Admittedly, the proposal seems to be well-intentioned, if the purpose is to reduce transportation emissions and to make people more aware of farming work. However, this could well be achieved through cleaner transport methods and by information campaigns in the media, rather than such drastic interventions in people's lives.

Overall, the idea is commendable in its ultimate objective of reducing pollution and increasing awareness. I feel, though, that the concept needs to be moderated into something much less severe, both to make it feasible and also to ensure that people support it.

(265 words)

Examiner's Comments

This essay has a well-organized argument against the stated proposal, beginning with an introduction which comments positively on the background and makes the opinion clear. The writer then deals with the two parts of the proposal, using good examples to debate against them. In this section, the candidate uses helpful phrases to introduce each stage of the argument: 'For one thing . . . To say that . . . As for the idea that . . .' The concession paragraph is also clearly introduced ('Admittedly. . .') and the conclusion summarizes the balanced opinion about the proposal ('commendable but needs to be moderated.') This is a comparatively short Task 2 essay, but the candidate has answered fully and with high quality English.

Certain phrases are used very naturally and effectively, especially when evaluating ideas:

An unviable idea (= impractical, unworkable, unfeasible)
An admirable concept
Unenforceable
Dystopian (= a highly negative imagined scenario)
Draconian measures (= extremely harsh actions by the authorities)
Drastic interventions (= severe interference)
A commendable idea (= praiseworthy, admirable)
To moderate a concept (= to reduce its severity)
Feasible (= practical, viable, workable)

Conclusion to Section Two

This concludes our section on personal viewpoint type essays. You have seen the ideal way to organize these essays, including the use of high-quality words and phrases to get your Band score as close as possible to a 9. In particular, you have seen how to present a nuanced or balanced opinion, using concessions and compromises in the 'concession' paragraph.

Remember, the discussion and personal viewpoint essays are asking for your opinion about something, but there are two other types of Task 2 essay which ask *not* for opinion but for your ideas and suggestions about a situation. These are the problem and solution type and the cause and effect type of tasks. Problem and solution type essays are the next section in this book.

Section Three: Problem and Solution Type Essays

Essay 17 (Topic: Cities and Infrastructure/Global Challenges)

Example Task

Many people in rural (countryside) areas hope to move to cities and settle there. What problems can this trend cause, and what solutions can you identify?

Explanation of the Task

This is a typical problem and solution type of task, which asks you to describe some problems or difficulties in a situation, and also to suggest some solutions to these issues. This type is very different from the discussion or personal viewpoint types, because the task is not asking if you think a situation is good or bad, or how much you agree or disagree with a statement. Instead of giving an opinion, you need to describe your ideas regarding problems and solutions in the situation.

The classic way to organize this type of essay is:

Short introduction paragraph which gives context or background (without an opinion.)

Main paragraph describing two or three problems in the situation

Main paragraph suggesting two or three solutions to those problems

Short conclusion paragraph summarizing the main paragraphs (without an opinion)

The following essay uses this structure to answer the task above, about rural migration.

Band 9 Model Essay

Migration from rural to urban areas is a frequent pattern in most countries, but the consequent problems can often be resolved by a careful response from the authorities.

Firstly, mass movement into cities can cause pressure on housing, leading to overcrowding and high rents. This can be unhealthy both physically and mentally, and the high costs can undermine the whole purpose of moving to the city (which is almost always economic.) Furthermore, people often arrive in cities without securing a job in advance, causing unemployment and possibly disorder if work is not found. Finally, of course, there is the impact on the rural areas left behind, which often suffer a lack of workers and infrastructure as the younger population migrates away.

To meet these challenges, the first priority should be better availability of housing at reasonable cost. This will usually involve cooperation between the city planners and private constructors, to build good quality accommodation in sufficient numbers (a process which must be safeguarded from corruption.) Secondly, to prevent workers arriving without jobs, a thorough program of job seeking could be started before the migrants leave the countryside, as is done in Brazil very effectively. This would match the workers' skills to what is needed in the city, allowing them to start earning immediately while doing productive tasks. Regarding the rural areas left behind, the authorities and employers ought to consider retraining those workers remaining, to ensure that important local work is prioritized and maintained, especially in the upkeep of basic infrastructure such as roads and irrigation.

In conclusion, the problems in both the cities and the countryside can be overcome by a proactive approach involving the authorities, businesses and, equally importantly, the migrants themselves.

(285 words)

Examiner's Comments

This Band 9 essay contains an appropriate number of ideas for both the problems and solutions aspects, and the layout is clear to follow overall and within the paragraphs. The introduction is short and makes a neutral comment about how widespread the problem is. The main paragraph giving three problems (housing, employment and left-behind countryside) is well signposted with 'Firstly . . . Furthermore . . . Finally.'

The solutions paragraph is similarly clear, and it is noticeable that all the sentences in both paragraphs contain more than a single idea. There is a clear link between each of the problems and each solution (sometimes candidates forget to connect them, which can reduce the Band score considerably.) The writer uses 'should/would/could/ought to' in this paragraph to make the suggestions, and this tentative language is a feature of academic English. The conclusion refers back to the problems ('cities and countryside') and paraphrases the strands of the solutions section.

There is some strong language to discuss problems and solutions:

Problematic
To cause pressure on something
To undermine the whole purpose of an action
To meet challenges
To safeguard a process (= to protect it)
Productive tasks
The <u>upkeep</u> of infrastructure (= maintenance)
To overcome problems
A <u>proactive</u> approach (= taking action without waiting to be asked)

Essay 18 (Topic: Global Challenges)

Example Task

The high cost of housing is an issue in many countries, especially for younger people. What problems might this cause for the people affected, and what solutions can you think of?

Explanation of the Task

A key concept in this Task is 'especially younger people,' so the essay will need to discuss the problems and solutions from their perspective mainly. Remember that you are not asked to give a personal view on whether the situation is an issue or not; the instruction assumes that the cost of housing *is* too high and asks you to imagine the problems caused, then suggest your solutions.

Band 9 Model Essay

The price of accommodation has been steadily rising in recent years, especially in cities where young people often want to live. Although this causes several problems, two solutions would probably help to improve the situation.

Possibly the main problem created is the difficulty people have in living where they wish, especially early in their careers when their incomes are lower. When urban housing is unaffordable, people move to outlying areas, pushing up prices there and adding the cost of commuting to their budget. Some younger people even miss out on promotions or job offers because of this, potentially affecting their careers. There is also the problem of overcrowding as people cram into shared accommodation, which we see in London for example, losing privacy and quality of life. A further impact is the delay in starting a family, because so much income is absorbed by housing payments. This can cause great unhappiness and it also suppresses the birth rate, which is the experience in Japan today.

To alleviate these problems, the authorities could expand the housing supply through a program of constructing suitable apartments for younger people to use. In addition, this scheme could reconfigure existing buildings, such as unused office blocks, into new accommodation. This could be financed jointly by the government and private developers. A second solution might be to reduce localized demand for housing by reducing the influx of young people to popular areas, for example by offering tax incentives to live in areas of lower demand, as has been tried in Australia with great success.

To conclude, young people are impacted in terms of their finances, careers and even their whole quality of life. Remedies should address the availability of housing stock and the demand for it in certain areas.

(292 words)

Examiner's Comments

This essay successfully describes problems from the position of young people, and then suggests solutions. The introduction makes clear that this will be the essay plan. The three ideas for the problems paragraph (location/overcrowding/starting a family) are all relevant and have good examples (London and Japan.)

The suggestions made in the second main paragraph connect to this by proposing changes to the location problem and expanding the housing stock generally. Both these points are focused again on younger people, with the example of Australia to support the idea. The conclusion manages to summarize all the ideas from the main section, using paraphrasing to avoid too much repetition.

The topic of urban problems and urban planning comes up frequently in the IELTS writing, reading and listening tests. This essay uses some excellent vocabulary on this subject:

Affordable/unaffordable housing
Outlying areas (= on the edges, comparatively distant)
To commute (= to travel a distance from home to work)
Overcrowding
To alleviate problems
To reconfigure buildings (= to transform for a new purpose)
An influx of people (= the continued arrival of a large number)
Tax incentives
Housing stock

Essay 19 (Topic: Work & Careers)

Example Task

In many countries, unemployment continues to be a problem in the rural (countryside) areas away from the big cities. What problems does rural unemployment cause? What solutions can be implemented by the authorities and by local businesses?

Explanation of the Task

This task asks you to think of solutions which can be achieved by two separate parties: the authorities and businesses. The best way to do this is to have two separate elements in the solutions paragraph, describing the two perspectives in turn. It is quite common for a Task 2 instruction to add an extra factor in this way, so it is important to practice dealing with this.

Band 9 Model Essay

Lack of work in the countryside tends to create huge challenges for local people and their economy. Local officials and private employers can nevertheless work together to find effective solutions, as I will explain here.

Perhaps the greatest problem is that unemployment often obliges people to move out of the area to find work elsewhere. This means that predominantly younger workers move away, leaving behind a depopulated area with older and less flexible workers still in place. Consequently, working patterns become less adaptable and more cautious, the local economy stagnates and a vicious cycle is formed, leading to more unemployment. A further problem is that lack of employment deprives the local authorities of tax revenues, meaning there is less investment in housing, infrastructure and facilities. Anyone who visits central France, for example, will see whole apartment blocks and sports stadiums abandoned due to lack of demand and funding.

Turning to solutions, the authorities could improve the situation by incentivizing workers to remain in the area through tax concessions or grants funded by national government. Although expensive, this would keep the local population stable and reduce unemployment by increasing local demand. Local businesses can play their part by training workers to a high level, thus increasing their skills and productivity. Finally, the authorities and businesses should partner together to capitalize on the local traditions and characteristics of the area, boosting interest in the region's identity. This is done in remote parts of Pakistan, for instance, with some success.

Overall, the destructive circle of rural unemployment can hopefully be broken by coordinated action involving employers and government in partnership, ideally building on a sense of local identity.

(276 words)

Examiner's Comments

The introduction makes clear that the candidate has understood the key point about authorities and employers, and introduces the theme of 'working together' which is picked up later. The 'problems' paragraph has a series of ideas which build on each other very effectively: 'Unemployment obliges people to move . . . This means that . . . Consequently . . . A further problem . . .' Candidates can raise their band score significantly by building ideas in this way. I am not sure if the example of France is accurate, but this ultimately doesn't matter because it supports the point being made. As examiners, we are not going to investigate the validity of the evidence and examples people use in Task 2, we just want to see clear and relevant ones.

The 'solutions' paragraph has a separate solution for authorities and businesses, and then the idea of partnership supported by an example. The conclusion summarizes the main ideas briefly.

I noticed some advanced and very natural phrases in particular which help raise the essay to Band 9:

Predominantly (= mostly, chiefly)
To stagnate (= to become static and unproductive)
A vicious cycle (= a situation where problems create further new problems)
Tax revenues/concessions
To capitalize on something
To boost interest in something (= to accelerate or drive upward)
A destructive circle
Coordinated action (= planned jointly by different people)

Conclusion to Section Three

This concludes our model essays on the problem and solution type tasks. You have seen how these essays are very different from the discussion and personal viewpoint type essays, requiring a different structure and techniques in writing them. You have also seen further useful vocabulary which you can use throughout your IELTS essays on all topics.

The next section deals with the cause and effect type tasks, which are similar in organization to the problem and solution type, but ask for a different set of ideas.

Section Four: Cause and Effect Type Essays

Essay 20 (Topic: Global Challenges)

Example Task

Many countries today suffer from crime in towns and cities. What are the causes of urban crime, and what effect does the situation have on local residents?

Explanation of the Task

Cause and effect type tasks have a similar structure to the problem and solution type, and the same principle applies. You should not give an opinion on whether something is positive or not, nor say whether you agree with the assumption given in the task. You need to think of two or three possible causes, and two or three effects. The paragraph structure should be the same as for problem and solution essays:

Introduction paragraph giving background (not opinion)

Main paragraph describing two or three causes

Main paragraph describing two or three effects

Conclusion paragraph summarizing the main ideas (not opinion)

In these essays, it is less important to connect the causes with the effects, because in reality there may not be a clear connection to be made. This is a big difference to the problem and solution type. In your planning time, the important thing is to think of relevant ideas for each main paragraph with examples and evidence.

The essay below answers the example task about crime in cities.

Band 9 Model Essay

City dwellers have to contend with a range of challenges, chief among which may be criminality in their neighborhoods. There seem to be three main causes of this problem and two major impacts.

Possibly the first cause of urban crime is drug abuse, meaning that addicts are desperate to obtain money by whatever means, and so lose respect for the law. There are also battles between rival drug distributors, some of which can escalate into deadly confrontations, as happens in Manila or Los Angeles. A further cause is overcrowding, which makes people hostile and aggressive to their neighbors and increases opportunities for petty crime such as the pickpocketing which is so prevalent in Paris and Rome. Finally, there is the problem of unemployment, which criminals often plead as the background to their behavior. While not all unemployed people resort to crime, of course, there appears to be a pattern here.

Turning to the impact of these crimes on local residents, one serious effect is financial loss due to theft or damage to property. This is often exacerbated by the high cost of insurance in cities, meaning that stolen goods such as bicycles or phones may not be insured. A further and equally damaging effect is the undermining of people's sense of security, as a result of constant exposure to threat and aggression. This can lead not only to low quality of life but even to mental health problems such as depression and paranoia. Sadly, this can in turn feed the cycle of conflict and instability.

In summary, we have seen that the key causes of urban disorder are drug abuse, overcrowding and lack of work. The main effects tend to be the toll both on people's finances and their psychological wellbeing.

(289 words)

Examiner's Comments

This essay is an ideal length for Task 2 and begins with a clear outline of what the content will be ('three causes/two impacts.') The first main paragraph uses 'First . . . Further . . . Finally . . .' to introduce its three ideas. The 'effects' paragraph fulfills the outline by presenting two impacts, and makes a strong point about the 'cycle of conflict.' The conclusion summarizes without repeating too much by using paraphrasing. This clear outline and organization make the essay very impressive. There is also a variety of vocabulary on show to describe difficult situations:

To contend with challenges
To escalate
Petty crime (= low level crime)
Prevalent (= common, frequent, used to describe problems)
To exacerbate a problem (= to make an existing problem worse)
Cycle of conflict

A toll (= a damaging effect or price)

Essay 21 (Topic: Nature, the Environment and Energy)

Example Task

There is widespread concern today about the damage done by humans to untouched areas of the world such as rainforests, mountains and coastlines. What are the causes of this situation, and what consequences might unfold now and in the future?

Explanation of the Task

This Task gives 'rainforests, mountains and coastlines' as examples of untouched areas in order to help you understand the context. You do not need to have a separate section for each of these sites, as they are just examples.

Tasks will sometimes use alternative words for 'causes' such as 'origins,' 'roots' or 'main reasons,' and other words for 'effects' such as 'consequences,' 'impacts' or 'repercussions.'

Band 9 Model Essay

We often see reports of harm done by people to prized natural sites, even in uninhabited areas. This essay covers the causes of this damage and its various impacts.

Probably the main cause is the expansion of human industry into previously untouched parts of the world. Examples of this are continued logging in Amazonia and gold mining in Africa and Australia, which affect rainforests, savanna and deserts. This damage is exacerbated by weak regulation and a lack of concern for nature by the companies involved. A further cause is the continued growth of tourism, especially by air, to ever more isolated destinations. These places are vulnerable to problems ranging from foot trampling to litter and waste, and there is often no plan in place to alleviate the damage.

Turning to the effects, the main impact at present is permanent landscape degradation, meaning that nature is treated so badly that it struggles to recover, as we see in the Amazon delta for example. The resulting landscape is either left in its damaged state, or may even be built over by developers, making any improvement impossible. A further effect is the damage to already fragile ecosystems; this habitat loss endangers wildlife and may potentially cause extinction of certain species. Looking to the future, a long-term consequence may be a threat to human existence itself, as the cumulative effect of both environmental destruction and species eradication undermines our food chains, potentially leading to famine and drought.

In conclusion, the causes of this crisis are human industry and tourism, while the effects involve landscape destruction, species extinction and possibly even a risk to human life.

(274 words)

Examiner's Comments

This Band 9 essay packs in a lot of ideas, but these are always clearly described with a variety of strong vocabulary. The organization is clear, with good paraphrasing of the concept in the Task and a confirmation that we are going to be describing causes and effects.

The 'causes' paragraph is very strong because the writer introduces ideas and then uses 'this/these' to refer back to the ideas and develop them:

'human industry . . . examples of this are . . . this damage is exacerbated . . .'
'tourism destinations . . . these places are vulnerable . . .'

This is a simple but very effective method of building up a main paragraph section. A similar structure is used in the 'effects' paragraph, which introduces each idea to guide the reader:

'Turning to effects . . . A further effect . . . Looking to the future . . .'

The conclusion is very brief, but nevertheless all the main ideas are summarized with some paraphrasing.

The environment is a frequent subject in all parts of the IELTS test, and this essay includes some common terms which candidates should be familiar with in order to gain a high score:

To exacerbate a problem
To alleviate a problem
Savanna (= extensive grassland)
To trample (to crush and damage under feet by people or animals)
Landscape degradation (= continued damaging decine)
Ecosystems
Habitat loss (= the places where animals naturally live)
Species eradication/extinction (= complete destruction, usually violent)
Food chains

Famine (= prolonged lack of food)
Drought (= prolonged lack of water)

Essay 22 (Topic: Global Challenges)

Example Task

There is widespread concern today at increasing levels of international tension and disputes between countries. What are the causes of these disputes, and what could the effects be?

Explanation of the Task

This is a potentially controversial topic, and so another example of an essay where you should avoid emotion and descriptions of personal experience, however strongly you feel. Note that 'tension and disputes' mean disagreements, not military warfare.

Band 9 Model Essay

International disputes continue to worry many of us, whether we are diplomats or private citizens. The origins of these conflicts and their potential impact can be extremely grave.

Probably the major cause of disagreements is disputed territory, where land is claimed by two different countries. These disputes often have roots going back for centuries, involving a clash of cultures which is more than merely political. Another cause is a shortage of commodities and raw materials, which make countries desperate to obtain certain goods whatever the consequences. This may be related to foodstuff, or to items such as computer chips and the metals needed to make them. A further flashpoint is often disagreement over trade and border controls, as we see in the continued friction between the UK and the European Union.

The consequences of this tension can be economic first of all, driving up the price of goods and materials as shortages occur and countries hoard supplies. This has knock-on effects within countries, as inflation provokes political upheaval and even the overthrow of constitutions, as Germany experienced in the 1930s. The effects can also extend to long-term hostility between countries, as governments begin to define themselves by their ability to confront certain foreign opponents or groupings. The final and worst outcome, of course, is an outbreak of war, which may begin as a localized conflict but can potentially draw in other nations and their armies.

Overall, the economic and cultural roots of such disputes are often historical or provoked by current crises. The effects can be economic, political and even military in nature.

(266 words)

Examiner's Comments

This Band 9 essay is clearly organized and has very relevant ideas and examples. The brief introduction puts the topic in some context and makes a comment about its seriousness. The first main paragraph has three logical ideas (territory, shortages, borders) and each idea is supported either by an explanatory comment or an example. The use of three ideas encourages the reader to expect three ideas in the next paragraph, and this is fulfilled with the ideas of economics, hostility and warfare. Again, each idea has a further comment which explains how it works and/or gives an example. This is a very effective structure which explains the ideas without using too many words. The short conclusion summarizes the main ideas.

I would highlight some useful vocabulary which can be used in Task 2 on any topic:

Extremely grave
A clash of cultures
Foodstuff (= raw materials for producing finished food products)
A flashpoint (= a source or moment where conflict starts)
Continued friction
To hoard supplies (= to keep supplies personally and not share)
Knock-on effects
Political upheaval (= confusing or chaotic changes)
Crises (= the plural of 'crisis')

Conclusion to Section Four

This concludes our section on the cause and effect type essays. Remember that the structure of these essays is similar to the problem and solution type, and these tasks are asking you for ideas about a situation rather than your opinion about it. These ideas-based tasks are the second most frequent in IELTS Task 2, after the opinion type tasks.

The least frequent type of Task 2 essay is the mixed type, in which the task combines elements from cause and effect, problem and solution, personal viewpoint and/or discussion types into one task. These tasks are rare, but the next section shows you examples of how to handle them if you meet one in the exam.

Section Five: Mixed Type Essays

Essay 23 (Topic: Children & Families)

Example Task

In many countries, there is concern that elderly and retired people are becoming increasingly isolated from the rest of society. What are the possible causes of this situation? What solutions can you think of to improve the situation?

Explanation of the Task

This task asks you to think of ideas, but these ideas are a combination of causes and then solutions. The structure of an essay like this should be:

Introduction (without opinion)
Main paragraph describing two or three causes
Main paragraph describing two or three solutions
Conclusion (without opinion)

Try to have two or three ideas in each of the main paragraphs, and avoid giving an opinion on whether something is good or bad. The following model essay answers the task above, about elderly people.

Band 9 Model Essay

Different cultures have different ways of relating to the elderly, but there is a global trend of increased separation from other people. The causes are complex, but we can also identify some solutions.

Possibly the main cause is a tendency for the elderly to self-isolate in the aftermath of the Covid pandemic, which is still a great concern for older people. This means that the elderly may not see their relatives very often, due to fears over infection and harm. Another cause is economic turbulence, which sometimes obliges people to move location seeking work. When this happens, their older relations are often left behind to fend for themselves. Although some can keep in touch electronically, this is a poor substitute for personal contact. A third cause is the hectic lifestyle which their younger relatives and friends may lead, meaning that they have little time available to reach out to the elderly.

Regarding possible solutions, we could start by improving healthcare available to this age profile, making services better and more affordable, so that anxiety over infection is less of a barrier. This would encourage the elderly to mix more naturally with others. We should also develop a new form of community center, places in which older people could meet with others their age, perhaps involving shared activities. These sites could be used for special events embracing the whole community, hopefully overcoming the absence of relatives which isolates them.

In conclusion, the causes of this sad situation are partly medical and partly economic, or connected to our busy lifestyles. Solutions may involve better healthcare and a fresh approach to community activities.

(270 words)

Examiner's Comments

This candidate has evidently understood that the task refers to causes and solutions. The introduction confirms this and comments on how widespread the issue is. The first main paragraph explains its ideas using 'This means . . . when this happens . . . meaning that . . .' The second main paragraph uses 'should/would/could' to propose solutions, which is a classic academic English style. The conclusion uses paraphrasing to summarize the main body's ideas.

There is some language here used very naturally and persuasively:

A global trend
Economic turbulence (= continued dramatic changes or fluctuations)
To fend for yourself (= to survive without any help or support)
A poor substitute
A hectic lifestyle (= uncomfortably busy)
A fresh approach
Overall, this essay gets Band 9 for its organization, clarity and language.

Essay 24 (Topic: Healthcare, Health & Sport)

Example Task

Many people today spend considerable time looking at screens, including computers, phones and other devices. What problems does this high level of screen time cause? What effects can it have on the users and people around them?

Explanation of the Task

This task mixes problems and effects, so it remains an idea-based essay in which you should think of ideas rather than give an opinion or agree/disagree. The main body should have two paragraphs giving two or three problems, then two or three effects.

This is another example of a task which gives some examples (computers, phones and other devices) to help you see the situation in context. As with essay 21 in this book, you do not need to create separate sections for computers, phones etc, but you could certainly use them as examples as the writer does in the following model essay.

Band 9 Model Essay

Electronic screens are such a universal part of life that it can be difficult for people to realise how much time they spend using them. High levels of screen use can produce various problems, and the consequences can be serious.

The major problems caused are firstly physical. This may involve back strain and poor posture if people are sitting at desks for long periods, and even repetitive strain injuries to their hands if they are typing constantly. Eyesight can also be damaged, both by desktop screens and by constant use of handheld devices such as phones and tablets. Opticians in Italy, for example, have noted a high incidence of sight deterioration among people who habitually watch entire films on their phones. We should add that excessive focus on a screen can also isolate the user from 'live' human interaction with friends, family and colleagues.

The physical effects of these problems can be manageable, with time off work or physiotherapy needed for strain injuries for example. However, eye problems can be notoriously difficult to reverse and can jeopardize the sufferer's ability to do screen-based work. This can ultimately threaten a person's entire career, with damaging effects for their finances and their families. The problem of isolation can also have long term consequences; people can become more comfortable with their screens than with real people, and thus grow increasingly withdrawn and socially inept. In the worst cases, this can even lead to mental health problems and personality disorders.

In summary, the problems involve strain of the body and eyes, and also social isolation. If allowed to accumulate, the effects can be deeply problematic and may even require specialist intervention.

(275 words)

Examiner's Comments

It is important that an ideas-based essay does not become a list of ideas, as sometimes happens. This particular Band 9 essay has a lot of sensible ideas which are built up without seeming like a list.

The introduction puts the issue in context and gives the outline of the essay ('various problems/serious consequences.') This helps the reader anticipate the next stages. The 'problems' paragraph introduces three problems and gives some commentary about each one. The 'effects' paragraph refers back to each of these ideas (strain, eyesight, isolation) and explains the possible consequences; this link between the two paragraphs is another way to prevent the ideas being just a list of bullet points. The conclusion is a very effective summary of the main body, which restates the point about the effects accumulating.

The candidate shows an excellent command of vocabulary both for physical conditions and for description of situations:

Poor posture (= the way your body is aligned)
Repetitive strain injuries
A high incidence of x (= a frequent appearance of x, used to describe problems)
Human interaction
Notoriously difficult (= well known for bad reasons)
Damaging or long-term consequences
Withdrawn (= introverted, unwilling to socialize)
Inept (= unskilled or clumsy at normal actions)
Personality disorders
Specialist intervention

Essay 25 (Topic: Culture, Art & Traditions)

Example Task

'You should take holidays (vacations) in your own country and get to know it fully, before going abroad as a tourist.' How far do you agree with this statement? Discuss the advantages and drawbacks of holidays in the home country, compared to going abroad.

Explanation of the Task

This task has the 'How far do you agree' element of personal viewpoint types, and also asks for a discussion of pros and cons like a discussion type essay. The best way to structure this essay is:

Introduction giving opinion supporting side A

Main paragraph supporting side B

Main paragraph supporting side A

Conclusion supporting side A

This will allow you to answer the task fully while coping with both the personal viewpoint and discussion aspects of the instructions. You could also have a concession element at the end of the second main paragraph, although this is not essential. The model essay below, about vacations, follows this layout.

Band 9 Model Essay

Anyone fortunate enough to have a vacation wants to use the time as fully as possible. Personally, I feel that going abroad (for those who are able) is preferable to staying at home, although there are good points to be made on both sides.

Regarding vacations in one's own country, these will usually be cheaper because travel expenses are lower, allowing one to perhaps take a longer break. There is also no language barrier, and so less risk of getting lost or stranded because of communication difficulties. In some countries, there is also a broad variety of destinations and landscapes available inside the country, meaning that there is less need to travel abroad for a change of scenery. In the USA, for example, half the population have no passport, because they are happy to vacation in America.

In my view, however, going abroad is a better choice. While more expensive, it will hopefully be better value for money, often because of the challenges one encounters in other languages and traditions. Learning to cope in another culture can be very rewarding, and the sense of achievement is substantial. We must remember, too, that not all countries have a range of possible destinations at home, and people are often obliged to travel abroad to find a particular feature. A Swiss person who wants a beach trip, for instance, will have to go outside their beautiful but landlocked country. I agree that people should get to know their own countries well, but this will usually happen naturally through work and study.

Overall, if a binary decision has to be made, I would opt for foreign travel, which is more challenging but ultimately more rewarding.

(281 words)

Examiner's Comments

This Band 9 essay does an excellent job of answering a difficult task by combining the elements of personal viewpoint and discussion clearly and logically. The introduction gives an opinion but also introduces the outline of discussing both sides. The first main paragraph has three ideas supporting home vacations (cost, language, variety) and these ideas are each responded to in the next main paragraph (value for money, sense of achievement, particular features.) This paragraph also makes a small concession to the case for home vacations. There is a clear link between the side of the debate supported in the second main paragraph and the opinion confirmed once again in the conclusion.

The examples used (America and Switzerland) are relevant, and support the debate well. The word count is ideal for Task 2. Some well-chosen vocabulary in this essay includes:

Travel expenses
Language barrier (= the inability to speak the local language)
A broad variety
Communication difficulties
A change of scenery
To encounter a challenge
A landlocked country (= with no sea coast)
A binary decision (= a decision with only two options)
Foreign travel

Conclusion to Book Three

You have now read twenty-five band 9 Task 2 model essays to help you improve your band score when you take the IELTS exam. We have shown you the different types of tasks, and the best way to organize and write essays in response to each one. Let's summarize the main points:

The most common task types are based on opinions: the discussion type and the personal viewpoint type. The next most common types are based on ideas: the problem and solution type and the cause and effect type. Occasionally, there will be a mixed type which combines elements from the other types. In the exam, make sure that you identify which type of task you are dealing with, and highlight the key concepts in the task instructions as we have done in the examples in this book. Then make a simple plan for your essay, following the structures we have explained.

Remember that, in opinion-based essays, you can 'pretend' to have a certain opinion in order to make the essay easier and quicker to write. There is no right or wrong answer to the opinion itself, the score is based on the structure of the essay and the quality of English used. In ideas-based essays, you need to express two or three ideas in each main paragraph, without giving a personal viewpoint or opinion on the situation itself. In all types of essay, your examples and evidence should come from things you know about in society generally, but not from stories about your personal life or people you know.

While this is fresh in your mind, we would recommend going back through the tasks in this book as soon as possible, and trying to plan and write your own essay in the forty minutes timing in answer to each of the tasks. Your essays will be different in content from the examples you have read, but we are confident that your writing will now be at a much higher band score than before you read this book.

We wish you the very best for your IELTS exam – and remember, the key to success is preparation and practice!

Book Four
IELTS Grammar Secrets

Book Four: IELTS Grammar Secrets

Introduction to Book Four

Getting a high band score (7 to 9) in IELTS writing is difficult even for people whose English is quite advanced. To achieve this result, you need to understand how to structure the different types of essays, how to use suitable vocabulary and how to use advanced grammar to convince the examiners that you deserve a high band. Surprisingly, however, many people take IELTS without researching how to write grammatically in Academic English. Unless you practice this, all your other hard work may well be wasted.

This book has ten modules which guide you through the principles of grammar in Academic English. Each module starts with an example Task 2 essay question like the ones you meet in the exam, then a Band 9 model essay, and three grammar topics showing you how to bring your own essays up to this band score. Each module then has a practice task for you to use the methods you have just learned. Try to write these practice essays as soon as you finish each module, while the methods are fresh in your mind.

By combining the grammar principles from all ten modules, you will make a huge difference to the examiner's assessment of your essay and so raise your band score. Thousands of people around the world have already used these methods to get the IELTS result they need and finally achieve their life goals – and you deserve to join them!

If you need a dictionary while using this book, we recommend the free *Cambridge Dictionaries Online* from Cambridge University Press.

Don't just trust to luck in your IELTS exam – the key is expert advice.

Jessica Alperne & Peter Swires
Cambridge IELTS Consultants
cambridgeielts@outlook.com

Frequently Asked Questions About Academic English

What is Academic English and why is it important?

This is the type of English used in formal writing for exams and essays everywhere in the English-speaking world. It is the type of English expected in IELTS Academic Writing Task 1 and Task 2. It will also be very useful for the IELTS General Training Writing Task 2, and help to raise your GT score substantially.

How is it different from normal, day-to-day English?

The vocabulary tends to be more formal, and the grammatical structures are much more complex. There are also high expectations of how you should present and explain your ideas, and the way that paragraphs and sentences are organised. This book explains these principles and shows you a wide range of examples.

What happens if I don't use Academic English in my IELTS Academic Writing test?

Unfortunately, it will be impossible to achieve over Band 6 unless you show a reasonable command of Academic English. Remember, your essay does not have to be perfect, but you must show the examiner that you understand the principles of Academic English and you have tried to use them. You may not remember all of the grammar methods from this book, but by using as many as you can you will increase your band score to get as close as possible to Band 9.

Do I have to use Academic English in the IELTS Speaking test too?

This question sometimes causes confusion. In the Speaking test, you should use the most advanced vocabulary you can, and give structured answers (see our 'Band 9 Speaking' e-book for full information about this.) However, you do not need to 'speak like an essay' or use formal words such as 'nevertheless' or 'moreover.'

Module 1

Structure - Conjunctions - Impersonal Style

Example writing Task

Some people believe that all children should have a pet or an animal to look after. Other people disagree, however, saying that this depends on a child's circumstances. Consider these opposing views, and give your own opinion.

Explanation of the Task

This is an Opinion > Discussion type Task. You should introduce the topic, discuss both sides of the argument, and give your opinion in the conclusion.

Band 9 model essay

It is often said that children benefit from caring for domestic animals, especially in today's technology-focussed world. However, the issue is not entirely straightforward, and arguments can also be made against the idea. This essay will discuss the debate, and give a concluding view.

On the one hand, those who support the ownership of pets cite the various benefits that the activity can bring to a child. These range from understanding nutrition, to learning about biology and daily routines. For example, food selection and exercise activities contribute to this strand of development, which adds greatly to a child's all-round education. Another argument is the emotional support that children receive from pets, meaning that the child feels more secure and thus more confident.

By contrast, opponents of this view point out that not all children live in a situation where pet keeping is advisable, or even possible. Examples can be seen in less affluent countries, where the expense of maintaining a pet may be prohibitive. In addition, many children live in unstable family environments, due to such issues as unemployment or political turbulence. For these families, pets would probably suffer neglect, meaning that it would be unfair to keep them, or possibly even dangerous. Finally, it must be said that not all young people actually want to keep a pet, because their interests lie elsewhere. For these youngsters, animal ownership should not be encouraged.

Overall, it seems advisable that the decision to keep a pet should be based on a child's interest, ability and family circumstances, rather than on a general view that 'all children' should have animals. It would appear that this serves the interests of both the children and the pets involved.

(278 words)

Module 1.1
Structure

This essay follows a classic Academic English structure for Opinion>Discussion Tasks, and the examiners will expect you to use something similar to this.

The introduction paragraph gives some background to the topic, and emphasises that this is an issue with differing arguments which the essay will consider. Because this is an Opinion>Discussion type essay, the candidate does not give an opinion in the first paragraph. Remember that in any Task 2 essay, two or three sentences are sufficient for the introduction.

The main body is divided clearly into two large paragraphs, each one presenting one side of the debate. Each paragraph has two or three ideas to support the view being presented. There is continuity between the second main body paragraph (which is against the universal keeping of pets) and the conclusion (which is also against this.) Because this is an Opinion>Discussion type essay, the candidate only gives his opinion in the final conclusion.

In the IELTS Academic test, this Task type is the most common, so you should practice following this model structure.

Module 1.2
Conjunctions

Conjunctions are linking words or phrases which connect ideas and sentences. This essay uses some of the most important academic conjunctions to inform the reader that the ideas are changing:

However
On the one hand
Another argument is
By contrast
In addition
Finally
Overall

There are also conjunctions to show that the ideas are being illustrated with examples:

These range from . . . to . . .
For example
Examples can be seen in

When writing this type of essay, try to keep these words and phrases in mind, and use them in the way that this model essay uses them.

Module 1.3
Impersonal style

In Academic English, it is possible to say 'I think/I believe/I feel' etc to give your opinion, if the Task asks for your view. However, you will increase your score if you show that you can use impersonal ways to express a view in the conclusion. 'Impersonal' means that you don't refer to 'I' but you use alternatives. This essay uses:

Overall, it seems advisable that
It would appear that

The examiner will recognise that you are giving an opinion in an academic, impersonal way, and will be impressed by this. In Opinion type essays, try to use one of the following phrases at least once, to express your view:

It seems that
It would seem that
It appears that
It would appear that
It is logical to conclude that
It is sensible to conclude that

Module 1 practice Task

The following practice Task is another Opinion>Discussion type Task, like the example we saw in Module 1. Try to write an essay for it in 250 words in about 40 minutes, using these Module 1 learning points about structure, conjunctions and impersonal style.

Some people feel that boarding schools (where students or pupils live at the school during the term) are an excellent option for children, while other people disagree for a number of reasons.
Consider both sides of this debate and reach a conclusion.

Module 2

Introductions - Conditionals - Tentative Phrases

Example writing Task

Many people today find that the cost of attaining a university-level education is extremely high for the students and their families. What are the causes of this situation, and how can governments, Universities and the students themselves overcome the problem?

Explanation of the Task

This is an Ideas>Mixed Task, asking for some ideas about the causes of a problem and also possible solutions. It does *not* ask for your opinion (for example, if you think that University is useful or worth the cost.) You should introduce the topic, suggest two or three causes, then two or three solutions, and then summarise.

The Task refers to solutions from *"governments, Universities and the students themselves"* and so you should think of an idea for each of these areas.

Band 9 model essay

While many young people aspire to attending University, the expense involved can be prohibitive in some cases. The causes of this appear to be focussed on three areas, and a number of solutions also appear to be possible.

Perhaps the major factor here is the reduction in government subsidy for University courses. For instance, in the UK, such courses were virtually free to the student until recently, but now cost around £30,000 per year. This pattern appears to be global, with the result that students and their families need to meet the costs directly. Another cause is the increasing cost of living in many countries, meaning that the cost of day to day life (in addition to fees) can be almost overwhelming for students. A third factor is the difficulty in finding part-time work while a student is studying. Such work tends to be poorly paid, while taking up time that students should use for their studies.

Turning to possible solutions, an obvious step would be to restore some element of state funding to courses. Although public budgets are under pressure these days, if we took this step it would greatly enhance access to courses for people on lower incomes. A second remedy might be for the Universities to offer shorter courses, or more courses with an element of professionally paid work experience included. If such courses were more available, it would reduce the issue of living expenses to some extent. Finally, students themselves should perhaps be more flexible in their attitude to education, and consider attending University at a later stage, or possibly only when they have accumulated sufficient funds to support themselves.

In summary, the factors of funding and cost of living appear to be the main causes. A coordinated response by the state, the institutions and the individuals may well lessen the severity of the situation.

(298 words)

Module 2.1
The introduction

In any essay, the first sentence of the introduction paragraph should give some general background information about the topic, and if possible say why the topic is important. The second sentence should make it clear to the examiner that you understand the type of essay the Task requires. The simplest way to do this is to outline the content of the main body, so that the reader knows exactly what to expect next.

This essay says:

The causes of this appear to be focussed on three areas, and a number of solutions also appear to be possible.

This emphasises to the reader that the main body will deal with causes and solutions. Another way to do this, using this Task, would be:

The origins of this situation seem to stem from three factors, while several remedies appear to be open to us.

Notice that the candidate is using impersonal phrases here (*seem/appear* and not *I think*) and also that the sentence does not take vocabulary directly from the Task question. It is important to paraphrase as much vocabulary as possible, to avoid duplicating from the Task.

Useful words to talk about causes of a situation are:

Origins
Roots
Factors
Underlying factors/causes

The factors stem from/derive from/flow from

Useful words for solutions include:

Remedies
Ways to solve
Methods to address/deal with
Answers to a problem

At the end of your introduction (a maximum of three sentences) the examiner should perceive that you understand the topic, and you have communicated what to expect in the main body.

<u>Module 2.2</u>
<u>Using conditionals</u>

When presenting possible solutions, it is traditional in Academic English to use the third conditional structure (If + simple past + would + verb.) This essay says:

If we took this step it would greatly enhance . . .
If such courses were more available, it would reduce . . .

This shows that the writer understands that she is discussing a hypothetical situation, and not a case that exists at the moment. Other examples of this are:

If governments were to ban smoking, this would affect . . .
If healthcare was cheaper, people could afford to . . .

When presenting solutions or recommendations, try to use this third conditional structure.

<u>Module 2.3</u>
<u>Tentative language</u>

'Tentative' means that you say that something might be true, or might happen, rather than saying that something is always true or always happens. This is important in Academic English because it shows you understand that situations are complex and there tend to be exceptions rather than 100% certainty in life.

There are many examples of tentative language in this essay (<u>underlined</u> here):

the expense involved can be prohibitive

Perhaps the major factor

the cost of day to day life (in addition to fees) can be almost overwhelming

Such work tends to be

A second remedy might be

students themselves should perhaps be

and consider attending University at a later stage

A coordinated response . . . may well lessen the severity

These expressions will achieve a much higher score than if you say *The expense is prohibitive/The major factor is/Such work is* and so on. This would be too simple to gain a very high score in IELTS.

In your essays, try to use this type of tentative language at least twice, to show the examiner that you understand it. For example, instead of:

The police should have guns, because this protects them

Try to say:

The police should consider having guns, because this tends to protect them.

Practice Task

Crime appears to be rising in most countries in the world, especially among young people. Identify the possible causes of this trend, and propose some solutions you think would be effective.

When writing this essay, try to use the learning from this Module about the introduction, using conditionals and tentative language.

Module 3

Concession - Linking Sentences - Academic Vocabulary

Example writing Task

It is often said that retirement is the happiest time of a person's life. How far do you agree with this view?

Explanation of the Task

This is an Opinion>Personal Viewpoint Task, asking if you support a given point of view. The structure is different from an Opinion>Discussion Task. You should introduce the topic, *give your opinion in the introduction*, and then explain your view. You should briefly consider the opposing view (this is called 'making a *concession*') and then restate your opinion in the conclusion.

Band 9 model essay

In many countries, the population is ageing consistently, and this presents the older people themselves with challenges as well as opportunities. It seems to me that retirement is not in fact the most contented period of life, and I will explain why in this essay.

Firstly, retired people have to contend with the major issue of health. No matter how optimistic a person is, and how conscientiously they try to keep fit, their health will inevitably decline as they grow older. This affects their mobility, their ability to interact with people, and their physical comfort when compared to the earlier stages of their life. A second negative factor is the whole question of finance. By this we mean that even people who have saved or invested carefully during their working lives will find their income in retirement reduced considerably, for example by relying on savings. This results in their leisure options being more restricted than in their younger years, even though they have more time to fill. This leads us on to the final, and perhaps most significant drawback to retirement, which is isolation. This happens when declining health and limited resources make people increasingly cut-off, even if they have surviving family members who seek to care for them. However much the family (or neighbours and social services) may offer support, this lack of contact will lead progressively to a less contented frame of mind.

It is true that there are some positives to retirement, most notably the time to pursue personal interests and the presence of grandchildren in many cases.

Despite this, it seems that for many older people, these pleasures are outweighed by issues which can cause stress and depression.

To conclude, the problems of health, financial concerns and isolation combine together to make retirement a challenging and potentially difficult time for many, especially when compared to the prime period of life. This is not to say that all retired people suffer in this way, but it appears to be the case very frequently.

(343 words)

Module 3.1
Concession

In this Opinion>Viewpoint type Task, you should give your opinion in the introduction. Most of the main body is then used to explain the reasons for your opinion. Notice that there is one large paragraph in the main body which does this.

After this large paragraph, there is then a smaller paragraph which describes the opposing point of view, and then rejects it. This smaller paragraph is called a concession. It is important to make concessions in Academic English, because without this the essay would be too unbalanced and one-sided.

This essay makes the concession by saying:

It is true that . . . (to describe the opposing view) . . . *Despite this* (to reject the view, giving a reason for rejecting it.)

Other useful phrases for making concessions and then rejecting the viewpoint are:

Admittedly . . . Nevertheless . . .
It might be said that . . . However . . .
I accept that . . . In spite of this . . .
While it may be correct that . . . It still appears to be the case, however, that . . .

In this type of essay, remember to have a small concession paragraph of two or three sentences after the large main body paragraph, using phrases similar to these.

Module 3.2
Linking the sentences

IELTS examiners often say that a common weakness in Task 2 essays is that sentences begin without any connection to the previous sentence. This makes the essay difficult to follow. In Academic English, it is important to link your sentences together. If you read the essay again, you will see some examples of how this is done:

decline as they grow older. This affects their mobility

the whole question of finance. By this we mean that

by relying on savings. This results in

more time to fill. This leads us on to

isolation. This happens when

grandchildren in many cases. Despite this

the prime period of life. This is not to say that

In these examples, the candidate uses the word *'this'* (or phrases with '*this*') to refer back to the previous sentence, helping the reader follow the progress of the argument. The sentences beginning with 'this' usually give a definition, an explanation or a development of the previous idea.

In your essays, especially in the main body, try to use 'this' phrases in this way. This applies to all types of Opinion and Ideas essays, because in all of them you need to give definitions, explanations or developments of your ideas.

Module 3.3
Academic vocabulary

In English, there are often two possible words for the same idea: an informal or neutral word (which is mostly Anglo Saxon in origin, such as 'often') and a more formal word (which is mostly Latin or French in origin, such as 'frequently.') In Academic English, we tend to use the more formal words, because they give the impression of professionalism and authority.

In this essay, the candidate has used a wide variety of formal/academic words. Here are ten of them, with the less formal alternative alongside:

Consistently (all the time = less formal)

Major (big)

Contented (happy)

Conscientiously (with a lot of care)

Decline (get worse)

Negative (bad)

Considerably (a lot)

Significant (big)

Pursue (go after)

Prime (best)

The IELTS examiners expect you to use this formal type of vocabulary rather than the very simple, less formal words such as 'big' or 'small.' The list of ten words above shows you some of the most frequent formal/academic words. You should definitely try to use most of these words in any Task 2 essay.

Practice Task

'Everybody should donate a fixed amount of their income to support charity.'

How far do you share this viewpoint?

Remember to use the points in this Module about concession, linking your sentences and academic vocabulary.

Module 4

Paragraph Structure - Using Evidence - Reporting Views

Example writing Task

Some people support the idea of imposing taxes on fossil fuels (oil, coal and gas) in order to reduce energy consumption. Others disagree with this approach. Consider the debate and its arguments, and come to your own conclusion.

Explanation of the Task

This is an Opinion>Discussion type Task. You should introduce the topic, discuss both sides of the argument, and give your opinion in the conclusion.

Band 9 model essay

Most people agree that the use of fossil fuels should be reduced to some extent. However, imposing taxes is a controversial tactic which appears to have a number of contradictory effects. We will consider both sides of the discussion in this essay.

On the one hand, those who support taxation of fossil fuels promote the idea that higher prices will lead to lower consumption and thus lower emissions. They point to evidence from countries such as Sweden where this appears to be the case, and urge other nations to follow suit. Furthermore, proponents of fuel taxes claim that the funds raised can then be used to subsidise renewable energy projects such as solar and localised biofuel reactors. To the supporters of the idea, these benefits are convincing.

However, opponents of fuel tax are able to cite evidence from other countries (including France and Italy) where higher tax has apparently not reduced demand for such fuels. In these cases, the effect has been to force people to pay more for the same volume of energy, which appears to penalise those who can least afford it. Moreover, critics of fuel tax also highlight the difficulty in governments promising renewable schemes without interfering in the entire energy market. If the state was to control the entire market for fuels, they say, this would force suppliers to leave the market, thus reducing competition and efficiency. This argument also appears to be quite powerful.

Overall, I would tend to side with the opponents of fuel taxation. It seems to be unreasonable to force vulnerable consumers to pay more for a commodity which is essential to them, without a real infrastructure for renewable energy being in place. It would be more logical to improve availability of renewables first, which would allow consumers to make a genuine choice.

(297 words)

Module 4.1
Paragraph structure

In any IELTS essay, the main body paragraphs must be carefully organised. The classic pattern is to have two or three ideas in each paragraph. If you have more than three ideas in each paragraph, you will probably not be able to finish the essay in forty minutes. This applies to all types of essay, both Opinion and Ideas types. In this essay, the candidate has used two ideas in each main body paragraph, to present the possible arguments on each side.

Notice how the ideas are presented: the writer uses a conjunction to introduce each idea (eg *On the one hand* or *Moreover*) and then states the idea, followed by a simple example and/or an explanation of the idea. Each idea is generally presented and/or exampled/ explained in two or three sentences:

On the one hand, those who support taxation of fossil fuels promote the idea that higher prices will lead to lower consumption and thus lower emissions. They point to evidence from countries such as Sweden where this appears to be the case, and urge other nations to follow suit.

When you are writing your main body paragraphs, try to organise them like this. Have two or three ideas, each idea being presented and/or exampled/explained in two or three sentences. Remember to use conjunctions to introduce the ideas.

Module 4.2
Using evidence

In the Task 2 instructions on the IELTS exam paper, the test tells you to 'use examples and evidence from your own knowledge and experience' (the exact words may vary, but the general instruction is always the same.) Remember that 'your own knowledge and experience' does not mean events that have happened to you personally or your friends and family. It means facts that you have read about in the media, or that you know from your own education.

In this essay, the candidate has used evidence from Sweden, France and Italy, but she has not given lots of statistics or numbers, which would be too detailed. In any Task 2 essay, try to use evidence in this way: refer to facts that you know about (not personal stories) and do not give too many statistics. In this way, your essay will be convincing and still easy for the examiner to read.

Module 4.3
Reporting views

When you are discussing different sides of an argument, it is a good idea to imagine how the supporters of one side would justify their views:

On the one hand, those who support taxation of fossil fuels promote the idea that . . .
Furthermore, proponents of fuel taxes claim that . . .
However, opponents of fuel tax are able to cite evidence . . .
Moreover, critics of fuel tax also highlight the difficulty . . .

By reporting other people's opinions in this way, your essay will be more interesting and the examiner will feel that you are able to balance arguments well.

Useful phrases to report views are:

Supporters of/ Proponents of/ Those who support x

Opponents of/ Critics of/ Those who oppose x

Supporters etc *cite/refer to/highlight/point to* x

Supporters etc *claim that/ say that/ insist that* x is correct

Supporters etc *deny that/ reject that/ do not accept that* x is correct

In your essays, try to use this type of 'reporting' method at least once in the main body.

Practice Task

Some countries today have passed laws against smoking tobacco in public buildings such as offices and restaurants. Other countries have no intention of doing this.

Consider the possible arguments on both sides of this debate, and reach your own conclusion on which side you favour.

Remember to use the points we studied in this Module about paragraph structure, using evidence and reporting views.

Module 5

Passives - Complex Adjectives - Cause and Effect

Example writing Task

Many countries today are experiencing problems associated with noise pollution (excessive noise above a normal background noise.) What are the causes of this phenomenon, and what effects does it have on the people affected?

Explanation of the Task

This is an Ideas>Cause/Effect essay. You should introduce the topic, then suggest two or three causes, plus two or three effects, and then summarise in the conclusion. Remember that this type of Task is not asking for your *opinion* (eg whether you think noise pollution is important or not) but for some *ideas* about causes and effects. Notice that this particular Task does not ask you to suggest any solutions.

Band 9 model essay

Noise pollution is a less-discussed form of pollution, but one which can have depressing effects on the people concerned. There seem to be two main causes, and a number of effects, which we will discuss here.

Possibly the main cause is the increased volume of traffic moving through and over our countries, especially the urban areas. The ever-rising use of road vehicles and aircraft leads to high noise levels throughout the day and night, which can be exacerbated by poor levels of sound insulation in homes, schools and other buildings. A further well-known cause is the amount of construction taking place, where roads and other facilities are built in rapid timescales. The use of machinery for this purpose results in decibel levels which can be dangerously high.

The effects of this problem on people can be quite serious. Firstly, increased stress levels are experienced because of the difficulty in thinking properly with high background noise. This can be especially damaging for children, whose academic performance can be affected in some cases. A further widely-observed impact is lack of sleep, which can be seen in cities which suffer noise pollution, such as London or Moscow. In these cases, local people start work tired and demotivated, which, in the case of workers who need high levels of concentration, can be dangerous for people around them. Finally, there is the long-term impact of depopulation, as people move away from flight paths and busy roads. Properties in these areas are often left derelict, or are taken over by squatters who then live in undesirable conditions.

Overall, traffic and construction seem to be the main causes, and they affect both individuals and the movement of population in the areas affected.

(290 words)

<u>Module 5.1</u>
<u>Passives</u>

. . . roads and other facilities are built in rapid timescales.

In Academic English, the use of passive structures like this is extremely important. The examiner will look for passives in your essay, and you will not be able to achieve over Band 7 unless you show that you can use them properly.

As a general rule, try to use a passive structure at least once in each paragraph of your main body, for every type of essay. It is not a mistake to say 'companies build roads' or 'people build roads' provided that you *also* show use of the passive.

Remember that you can use the passive in any tense:

Roads were built in the nineteenth century.

Roads have been built since the 1800's.

Roads are being built these days.

Roads will be built to meet demand.

And so on.

<u>Module 5.2</u>
<u>Complex adjectives</u>

Complex adjectives have an adjective plus another word (frequently an adverb), such as in this essay:

A <u>less-discussed</u> form

The <u>ever-rising</u> use

A well-known cause

A widely-observed impact

A long-term impact

These phrases are usually written with a hyphen (-) although you may read some books or articles where the writer does not use a hyphen. Using complex adjectives like this shows the examiner that your Academic English is advanced and you have a wide range of vocabulary. Other useful complex adjective phrases are:

There should be a wide-ranging discussion about . . . (= a discussion covering many topics)

The ever-present danger of . . .

X is a much-discussed problem.

X is a constantly-evolving field of research.

There is a widely-held concern that . . . (= many people share this concern)

Many long-established traditions have been lost.

You do not need to use these complex adjectives all the time, of course, but try to use at least one in your Task 2 essay.

Module 5.3
Cause and effect

You will need to discuss causes and effects in an Ideas>Cause/Effect type essay, but the language involved is useful for all the other essay types as well. This essay shows you some of the most common phrases. Some of the other useful ways to describe causes and effects in Academic English are:

X causes Y

X leads to Y

X results in Y

X brings about Y

X contributes to Y (= it is not the only cause)

X affects Y

X has an effect on Y (remember that *an effect/to affect* are spelled differently)

X impacts (on) Y/ X has an impact on Y

X exacerbates Y (= makes a problem worse)

X undermines/weakens Y (= makes it weaker)

X damages Y

X lessens Y (= makes it smaller or less frequent)

X improves Y

X ameliorates Y (= makes a problem better for the victim)

These are all formal, academic phrases which the IELTS examiners will be pleased to see in your Task 2 essay.

Practice Task

Illiteracy continues to be a concern for many countries in the world today. What are the causes of illiteracy in the modern world, and what effects does it have on the people concerned and on society as a whole?

Remember to practise the language we have studied in this Module, and use passives, complex adjectives and phrases for cause and effect.

Module 6

Avoiding Emotion - Evaluating Evidence - Noun Persons

Example writing Task

'Healthcare should always be funded by governments, and it should always be free for people to use.' To what extent do you agree or disagree with this idea?

Explanation of the Task

This is another Opinion>Personal Viewpoint Task.

You should introduce the topic and give your opinion in the introduction. The main body should explain your view, giving two or three reasons. You should briefly consider the opposing view ('making a concession') and then restate your opinion in the conclusion.

Band 9 model essay

Few topics are more important than a nation's healthcare, and the issue of payment will probably always be controversial. It seems to me that the sheer cost of universal, free healthcare makes this an impractical aspiration, no matter how much we might admire the idea.

The main obstacle would appear to be the number of recipients of healthcare compared to the taxpayers are who need to fund it. Especially in countries with ageing populations such as Europe, the tax burden on workers becomes intolerably high, and can eventually stifle economic growth. These painful lessons, shown by states such as France, seem to demonstrate that completely free healthcare is economically unsustainable. A further issue relates to the cost of modern medicines, which can be extremely high if the latest drugs are used by health providers. This means that the cost of providing treatment rises almost without limits, making the permanent supply of free treatments unaffordable. One final point against this proposal is the added issue of globalisation, by which people move increasingly freely between countries. If this means the taxpayers of one nation are now obliged to fund the healthcare of users from many other nations, this is surely a further significant factor which clearly makes a universal health service impractical.

Admittedly, I agree with those who argue that free a health service is a worthy ambition for a country to have, and that we should all contribute something to the welfare of our fellow citizens. However, this aspiration suffers significantly when confronted with financial reality.

To summarise, it seems reasonable for the state to fund as much as possible of the nation's healthcare. However, due to demographics and costs, this needs to be supplemented by other methods, such as private insurance.

(288 words)

Module 6.1
Avoiding emotion

It is an important feature of Academic English that the writer does not use emotion or humour. Even if the topic is one that you feel strongly about, there are ways to show how you feel without using emotion.

For example, it would be wrong to write something such as:

Free healthcare is a wonderful/brilliant idea

Free healthcare is a terrible/ludicrous idea

Words such as this are too emotional and should never be used in IELTS academic writing, even though we may use them in conversation.

In this essay, the writer shows his strong feeling for or against an idea by using unemotional phrases such as:

the sheer cost (= the cost is very high and is a factor by itself)

an impractical aspiration (= would not work in reality)

the tax burden on workers becomes intolerably high (= people would not accept it)

These painful lessons (= causing serious problems)

unaffordable (= cannot be afforded)

this is surely a further significant factor (= most people would agree with me)

If you use vocabulary such as this, the IELTS examiner will recognise that you have a strong opinion and you are expressing it in a professional, academic way. Other useful academic phrases to express a strong opinion include:

This idea would surely be unacceptable to most people (= most people would disagree strongly)

It cannot be denied that/ It is undeniable that . . . this idea is positive/helpful/imaginative etc (= I think this and most people would agree.)

It is an inescapable fact that . . . (nobody can say this is not true.)

The benefits of this approach appear to be overwhelmingly positive. (= so positive that most people would support it.)

This concept seems to be somewhat inadequate. (= not really good enough for its purpose.)

It is almost universally accepted that . . .

There is an almost universal consensus that . . .

In Opinion type essays, try to use vocabulary such as this at least once when you give your opinion. The examiner will give you marks for avoiding emotion and using advanced academic language.

Module 6.2
Evaluating evidence

In Module 5, we saw the method of presenting an idea and then giving an example or explanation as evidence. In this essay, look again at the way the writer evaluates the evidence. 'To evaluate' means to give a judgement on something compared to other things. Some examples from this essay are:

These painful lessons, shown by states such as France, seem to demonstrate that completely free healthcare is economically unsustainable.

The candidate uses 'seem to demonstrate' to emphasise that the evidence supports his view.

This means that the cost of providing treatment rises almost without limits, making the permanent supply of free treatments unaffordable.

The candidate uses 'This means that . . . making . . . + adjective' to explain how the evidence is another example of his argument.

. . . this is surely a further significant factor which clearly makes a universal health service impractical.

The candidate uses 'clearly makes' to evaluate (= give a judgement on) the evidence he presents.

However, this aspiration suffers significantly when confronted with financial reality.

In this concession paragraph, the candidate uses 'However' to introduce a rejection of the opposing idea.

Try to use *demonstrates/means that . . . making/clearly makes* and suitable conjunctions to comment on the evidence you present and explain how and why the evidence supports your argument.

Module 6.3
Noun persons

'Noun persons' are nouns used to identify people by their role in a situation. For example in this essay, we have:

taxpayers
workers
health providers
those who argue that

This is a frequent method in Academic English, because it avoids the use of 'people' (*'people who pay tax/work/provide health/ people who argue that'* etc)

Other very frequent noun persons useful for IELTS essays are:

Those who support x/Those who oppose x

Those who accept x/Those who reject x

The authorities (= the government, police and courts)

Contributors to x

Recipients of x

Observers (= journalists and analysts who comment on situations)

Researchers

It is not a mistake to say 'people who + verb.' However, as always in IELTS academic writing, to achieve a high score you must show that you can use at least some of the noun persons explained here.

<u>Practice Task</u>

'All children should learn to speak a foreign language as soon as they start school.' How far do you agree with this proposal? How important is it for a child to learn a foreign language?

Remember to practise using the language for avoiding emotion, evaluating evidence and the noun persons that we have seen in this Module.

Module 7

Rejecting Arguments - Topic Vocabulary - Conclusions

Example writing Task

Should companies (businesses) ensure that they employ a quota (or fixed percentage) of women in all jobs, or is this an impractical concept?

Discuss both sides of this debate, and reach a conclusion based on your own opinion.

Explanation of the Task

This is an Opinion>Discussion type Task. It asks you to focus in particular on the key word 'impractical' and to consider whether or not the 'quota/fixed percentage' idea is impractical (*impractical* = it would not work in reality.)

You should keep this in mind when discussing both sides in the main body.

Band 9 model essay

Workplace quotas have been suggested for some time now, in an attempt to encourage gender equality in the workforce. The idea provokes strong arguments, which I will consider here.

On the one hand, it can be said that quotas would allow women to enter traditionally male professions, ranging from surgeon to airline pilot. This, it is argued, would expand the pool of people available to do these jobs, and reduce inequality between the sexes. Furthermore, supporters of quotas claim that the procedure would encourage women into the workforce generally, thus increasing family incomes and improving the standard of living of many people and families.

The other side of this debate is that gender quotas may simply be unenforceable in practical terms. This is because the number of women who wish to be (for instance) airline pilots or surgeons appears to be substantially lower than the number of men. This being the case, it would appear to be impossible to enforce a quota in many areas. A second point is that a quota should logically work for both genders, and thus men would have to be employed in traditionally female roles such as primary teaching or nursing. Again, we would find ourselves asking men to take on jobs which they are not inclined to do. A final point is that the reduction of inequality should start at an early age, with equality of qualifications, career and life choices, rather than being enforced retrospectively by employers or the state.

To conclude, it appears that the aim of these quotas is admirable, but they are unworkable in realistic terms due to the differing wishes of the existing workforce. A longer-term and more thoughtful programme is surely needed.

(284 words)

Module 7.1
Rejecting arguments

In the first main body paragraph, the candidate presents some ideas in favour of the 'quota' idea. In the second main body paragraph, the candidate addresses the point about the 'impractical' instruction in the Task. He presents three ideas against the 'quota' and then gives examples and explains why each idea means that the idea is not really practical. He uses the third conditional to *imagine the consequences* of implementing the idea:

. . . men would have to be employed . . .
. . . we would find ourselves asking men to take on jobs . . .

He also uses the tentative language which we studied in Module 2 in order to show that he understands the situation is complex, and he is basing his arguments on careful evidence:

quotas may simply be unenforceable

appears to be substantially lower than

it would appear to be impossible to enforce

it appears that the aim of these quotas is admirable

Notice also that he uses 'surely' to show that he has a strong opinion without using emotion:

. . . programme is surely needed.

In a 'Discussion' type essay such as this, you may find it useful to use the second main body paragraph to reject the argument in the first main body paragraph, using the type of language explained here.

Remember that your view in the second main body paragraph should connect with your view in the conclusion. For example, if this candidate felt that quotas are in fact *practical*, he would have this argument in the *second* main body paragraph, connecting with his conclusion which would be in favour of quotas.

Module 7.2
Topic vocabulary

All IELTS Task 2 Academic Tasks relate to a small number of topics which appear throughout the IELTS exam. These topics are:

Work

Education

Children and families

The environment and energy

Culture, art and traditions

Health and sport

Global and social problems

Cities and the countryside, including infrastructure and agriculture

Government and the authorities

Task 2 will never ask you to comment on specifically detailed scientific or technical issues (except issues which are of general interest, such as space exploration or GM crops.)

It is useful for you to have in mind just a few words and phrases relevant to each of these topics, so that you can show the examiner you have a strong range of topic vocabulary.

In this essay (which is on the Work topic) the candidate uses:

Workplace
Workforce
Professions
Roles

Equality/inequality

Using this small number of topic-specific words in Task 2 will improve the credibility of your essay considerably. Here are some other key topic-specific words which are very useful for Task 2:

Education: formal education, higher education, syllabus, curriculum, testing

Children and families: nuclear family, extended family, role model, upbringing, child development

The environment and energy: emissions, fossil fuels, greenhouse gases, renewable energy, subsidies

Culture, art and traditions: folklore, handicrafts, fine art, mythology, rituals

Health and sport: obesity, sedentary lifestyle, fitness, spectator sports, competitiveness

Global Challenges: unemployment, endangered species, erosion, deforestation, natural habitat

Cities and the countryside, including infrastructure and agriculture: urban sprawl, depopulation, rural migration, transport hubs, facilities

Government and the authorities: the courts, sentencing, policy, initiative, programme

Of course, there are many more words and phrases relevant to these IELTS topics. As you are reading IELTS practice papers or the general media, make a note of vocabulary relevant to these topics and try to remember them. If you can use just a small number in your essay, the examiner will raise your score.

Module 7.3
Conclusions

In any Task 2 academic essay, the conclusion paragraph should be a maximum of three sentences (two sentences are usually enough.)

You should try to summarise the main ideas from the main body, but you should paraphrase (= use words which mean the same) so that you do not repeat vocabulary. In this essay, the candidate has paraphrased from the main body (main body words in brackets):

To conclude, it appears that the aim (an attempt) *of these quotas is admirable, but they are unworkable in realistic terms* (unenforceable in practical terms) *due to the differing wishes of the existing workforce.* (jobs which they are not inclined to do.) *A longer-term* (start at an early age) *and more thoughtful programme is surely needed.*

When writing your conclusion, remember that you should not include any new ideas or evidence, but only summarise and paraphrase the main body ideas.

Practice Task

In many countries, old or traditional languages are dying out or being forgotten, especially by younger people. Is this an acceptable development which occurs inevitably, or is it something which we should try to prevent?

Practice using the ideas from this Module about rejecting arguments, topic-specific vocabulary and conclusions.

Module 8

Problems - Solutions - Time and Probability

Example writing Task

Many people today find they have insufficient time to spend with their families, because of pressures of work. What problems does this create for individuals and their families? What solutions can you propose? Which would be the most effective solution, in your view?

Explanation of the Task

This is an Ideas>Problem/Solution type essay. You should introduce the topic, then give two or three problems, two or three solutions, and then summarise in the conclusion. Notice that the Task asks you to think about *individuals and their families*, and also to identify *the most effective solution.*

Band 9 model essay

Excessive time spent at work can ultimately take a serious toll on workers and their families in various ways. We will discuss the most serious problems arising, and also two ways in which the situation can be improved.

Arguably the gravest problem caused by overwork is the stress that the workers themselves suffer from. When a person is working long hours, and thinking about work even outside that time, the ability to relax is severely curtailed. This can rapidly lead to physical exhaustion and mental anxiety, which eventually undermine the victim's overall wellbeing. A further serious impact is the disruption to family relationships, especially with a spouse and children. Family members may soon become accustomed to the absence of a father or mother, damaging the natural bonds which bind a family together and potentially eroding the security of the family unit itself. The long-term consequent problems of family breakdown may include depression, poor self-esteem and academic underperformance.

To counteract these dangers, perhaps the most effective and most immediate solution would be for employers to incorporate a fixed amount of free time into their workers' schedules. For example, companies might commit to a 'no work, phone calls or emails after five pm' policy, as is being suggested in Germany at present. This would lessen the anxiety of high workloads and preserve family time. Another remedy may be to promote the use of relaxation techniques among workers, so that they make the most of the free time that they have. Activities ranging from sport to yoga or family events can be used to maximise any opportunities for de-stressing that already exist.

In conclusion, the main problems seem to be stress and potential family breakdown. The key solution would be the formal protection of leisure time, together with better use of it by workers themselves.

(302 words)

Module 8.1
Problems vocab

You may need to explain the problems in a situation in any Task 2 essay. This essay shows some of the classic Academic English ways to describe problems:

. . . the gravest problem . . . (= most serious)

. . . the ability to relax is severely curtailed (= restricted, limited)

This can rapidly lead to . . .

. . . undermine the victim's overall wellbeing. (= make weaker)

A further serious impact is . . .

. . . disruption to . . . (= breaking up an ordered system)

. . . damaging the natural bonds . . .

. . . potentially eroding the security . . . (= gradually removing)

The long-term consequent problems . . . may include . . .

Other useful phrases to discuss problems are:

X destroys Y
X eliminates Y
X makes Y deteriorate (= become worse)
X dilutes Y (= makes it weaker, less focussed)

Other words which can be used to paraphrase problem include:

Crisis
Issue
Question
Concern
Anxiety
Challenge

Almost any Task 2 essay will need to use some of these phrases, especially for Tasks which ask about situations which could be negative for people or society.

Module 8.2
Solutions vocab

The second main body paragraph in this essay shows some useful ways to present and explain solutions:

To counteract these dangers (= fight against)

This would lessen the anxiety of (= reduce)

Another remedy may be to (= solution or step)

To maximise opportunities (= to make the most of)

Other useful words which can be used to paraphrase *solutions* are:

Measures
Steps
Initiatives (= a new idea, usually from the authorities)
Policies
Programmes

Useful phrases to talk about how solutions work include:

To penalise people for doing X (= to make them pay a penalty for it)
To ban or outlaw X (= to make it illegal)

To curb/restrict X
To prevent people from doing X
To promote or encourage X
To raise awareness of X
To force/oblige people to do X

Try to use these academic words, rather than say *We should stop people doing X* or *We should get people to do X*, which is too simple to achieve a high score.

Module 8.3
Time and probability qualifiers

This essay uses some effective language to talk about the probability of something or the timescales in which things happen:

ultimately (= eventually, finally)
rapidly
soon
potentially
long-term
immediate

It is easy to include some of the qualifiers in your ideas, to show that you have thought about the probability and/or timescales of the events.

Other typical examples of these words are:

X may possibly happen

X will inevitably happen (= it cannot be prevented)

X will undoubtedly happen

X will gradually/steadily happen

X will happen step by step

X will suddenly happen

X will spontaneously happen (= without outside help)

In your essays, try to include some of these qualifiers; this is a straightforward way to improve the examiner's perception of your writing.

Practice Task

The use of violence in music lyrics, video games and films seen by children is causing concern in many societies. What problems may be caused by this type of violent imagery, and what steps could be taken to lessen the impact on young people?

Remember to include the language in this Module for problems, solutions and time/probability qualifiers.

Module 9

Disadvantages - Alternatives - Collocations

Example writing Task

'The key to reducing crime is to have more police patrolling the streets.' How far do you support this proposal? What other ways of reducing crime may be effective?

Explanation of the Task

This is another Opinion>Personal viewpoint Task. It asks you to agree or disagree with the proposal, and also to suggest some alternative methods. The IELTS writing test sometimes adds an extra element to the Opinion Tasks in this way.

You should introduce the topic, state your view, explain your view and then suggest some alternatives, finishing with a summary conclusion that restates your view.

Because of the extra element in the Task, the examiner will not object if you do not have a concession paragraph in this particular essay.

Band 9 model essay

We are all concerned about high crime levels and possible ways to reduce crime, especially in cities. The idea of having high numbers of visible police officers may be initially appealing, but some analysis will show that it is not the key method and that other options are preferable.

Firstly, we should ask what the purpose of extra police in public would be. It is probably true that this tactic would reduce minor crime such as littering and unsocial behaviour, but determined criminals such as thieves and muggers will inevitably find ways to operate despite the police presence. The example of New York shows that police patrols initially reduce crime to some extent, but crime then levels off and persists at the lower rate, no matter how many more police are added. Secondly, it must be said that many crimes which worry the public today, such as identity theft or financial hacking and fraud, are not carried out on streets and thus would be invisible to police patrols anyway. This means there is a danger that we would be responding to a current threat with an outdated tactic.

Turning to possible alternatives, probably the most effective would be to improve the efficiency of existing police rather than increase their numbers, for instance by better training in computer-based crime. This would generate improved rates of detection for crimes and more efficient use of the vast amount of technology available. Another viable option would be to increase penalties for criminals, which would have the benefit of deterring them from committing crime at all. Both these alternatives would be comparatively cheap, and would address the root of the problem rather than seeking to suppress the symptoms.

Overall, we have seen that increased patrols are of limited effectiveness because they are superficial in nature. Better training and stronger sentencing would appear to be far more robust alternatives these days.

(314 words)

Module 9.1
Presenting disadvantages

In this essay, the candidate points out the disadvantages of some ideas:
It is probably true that . . . but . . .

Secondly, it must be said that . . . and thus would be . . .

This means there is a danger that we would . . .

Other ways to present the disadvantages of an idea are:

It may be true that X is cheaper; nevertheless, in the long term it would be a more expensive option.

While X may have some advantages, these appear to be outweighed by the costs . . .

It might initially appear desirable to do X, but on closer inspection the idea suffers from several problems.

There seem to be a number of drawbacks associated with X, the most significant of which is . . .

Notice that when writers discuss disadvantages, they often begin by conceding that there are some small advantages (*It may be true that* . . . for example.) This helps the essay appear very balanced and objective, especially in this example where there is no concession paragraph. Try to do this at least once when you are explaining the disadvantages of an idea or proposal.

Module 9.2
Presenting alternatives

Task 2 frequently asks you to suggest some alternative ways of achieving something. It is best to present these alternatives in a smaller, self-contained paragraph after the main body. If you try to put your alternatives in the main body ideas, the essay will probably become confusing for the reader.

This essay shows you the importance of using a conjunction phrase to introduce the paragraph presenting the alternatives:

Turning to possible alternatives, probably the most effective would be . . .

This helps the examiner to expect what is coming next. Other ways to introduce a paragraph giving alternatives are:

Regarding other possible options, . . .

If we now consider other ways to do this, . . .

On the subject of alternatives, . . .

Of course, there are also alternatives, including . . .

You should then give examples and explain the alternatives, as you would do with ideas in the main body. Some useful ways to introduce two or three possible alternatives are:

Another possible option would be to do X, which would achieve . . .

A further possibility seems to be X, which might achieve . . .

Alternatively, we could also do X, which would have the effect of achieving . . .

In the exam, make sure you read the Task instruction carefully to check whether it is asking you to suggest alternative ways of doing something. This might be included at the end of the instructions for both Ideas and Opinions type essays.

Module 9.3
Collocations

A 'collocation' is a set of words which traditionally are used together. Examples from general English are 'extremely happy' and 'deeply disappointed.' In IELTS writing, you will increase your score if you can use some of the Academic English collocations which are used in formal writing. This essay has some good examples:

minor crime
to some extent
current threat
possible alternatives
improved rates
viable option
suppress the symptoms
limited effectiveness
robust alternatives

By using these colocations, the writer shows that she can write in the formal, academic style used in business, colleges and universities. Some of the other very frequent academic collocations which you should use in your IELTS essays are:

There is widespread concern about . . .
It is virtually certain that . . .
It is barely conceivable that . . . (= it is very hard to imagine this happening)
There is universal consensus that . . . (= everybody agrees on this)
It is of paramount importance that . . . (= maximum importance)
It seems highly likely/unlikely that . . .
It is generally accepted that . . .

Try to use these colocation phrases wherever possible in your essays, and the examiner will recognise that you are using advanced Academic English.

Practice Task

'The best way to educate children is by using the Internet in every lesson.'
To what extent do you share this opinion? What other ways are there of making lessons effective for children?

Try to practice the lessons from this Module regarding presenting disadvantages, alternatives and using collocations.

Module 10

Complex Sentences - Academic Phrases - Conclusions

Example writing Task

It might be said that protecting the environment is the most important challenge facing governments today. How important do you feel this issue is? Are there other challenges which are of equal or greater importance?

Explanation of the Task

This is an Opinion>Evaluate type essay. You should introduce the topic, say how important the topic issue is, and then explain why you think that other issues are more (or less) important. The conclusion should be a brief summary of the main points.

Band 9 model essay

Environmental issues are a concern for almost everyone today, as we see the natural world suffering increasing damage from pollution, construction and other human activity. However, to say that governments should regard this one issue as their main priority may be a rather simplistic view.

Admittedly, it is correct that environmental protection should be among our greatest concerns. Without coordinated measures from national and global organisations, the environment will continue to deteriorate, leading to a more unstable world for us all. However, by focussing on this topic to the exclusion of others we run the risk of neglecting a range of other, equally grave challenges.

Foremost among these other challenges appears to be the question of overpopulation, by which I mean the growth of human numbers beyond the ability of the human race to support itself. If this problem is not addressed, we potentially face the collapse of modern human society, and consequently the ability of the human race to combat the environmental damage which has already taken place. Another challenge which is at least equal to the environment is the need to reduce poverty and disease in less developed countries, which again would enable those populations to play a larger part in attempts to preserve nature. Finally, there is the question of unemployment and the need to find ways to reduce this problem. By increasing the number of people in work throughout the world, governments would create the revenues and economic stability required to make environmental protection more viable.

Overall, the environment is certainly a major priority. However, it should be seen as one among a range of issues to be solved, and the solutions themselves could lead to better preservation of nature.

(284 words)

Module 10.1
Complex sentences

A complex sentence simply means a sentence with two or more ideas contained in it. One of the most common weaknesses which IELTS examiners say they find in essays is that *all* the sentences are too short or too basic. In this essay, the candidate has shown several times that, although some of his sentences are quite short, he can also use complex sentences such as these:

Without coordinated measures from national and global organisations, the environment will continue to deteriorate, leading to a more unstable world for us all.

Foremost among these other challenges appears to be the question of overpopulation, by which I mean the growth of human numbers beyond the ability of the human race to support itself.

Using *leading to* and *by which I mean* are good ways to show the examiner that you can write complex sentences.

Other useful ways to build these sentences are:

While X may be positive in some respects, we should also consider its negative aspects, namely A, B and C.

We face a number of challenges in this field, ranging from A to B and even, in the long term, C.

We should not only do X, but also consider doing Y as well.

Although it may be useful to do X, this would result in Y, causing . . .

In any IELTS essay, try to make sure that the *majority* of your sentences are complex ones. Remember that using *leading to/causing/resulting in* is often the easiest way to do this.

Module 10.2
Academic phrases

Just as academic collocations (sets of words which traditionally go together) show that your writing is advanced, there are also some academic phrases which are widely used. This essay uses:

It is correct that . . .

. . . by focussing on this topic to the exclusion of others . . .

. . . we run the risk of . . .

Foremost among these other challenges . . . (= the most important)

. . . one among a range of issues . . .

Other useful academic phrases for you to use include:

By no means (= certainly not)
Eg Pollution is by no means the only challenge that we face (= pollution is certainly not the only one)

Above all (= the most important or most urgent thing)
Eg *Above all, we must try to reduce crime, because . . .*

Regardless of (= it does not matter)
Eg *Governments should create a high quality transport infrastructure, regardless of the cost* (= the infrastructure is so important that the cost does not matter)

By this we mean that . . .

This is not to say that . . . (= this does not necessarily mean that . . .)
Eg *Crime is a major concern, but this is not to say that it should be the only focus for the authorities.*

Try to remember these phrases, and use them at least twice in your Task 2 essay. If you use them correctly, the examiner will give you credit for using Academic English.

Module 10.3

Conclusions

In Task 2, always try to write a balanced conclusion. This means that your summary or conclusion recognises that a situation is complex, and that a number of factors are involved:

Overall, the environment is certainly a major priority. However, it should be seen as one among a range of issues to be solved, and the solutions themselves could lead to better preservation of nature.

This is more in the tradition of Academic English than saying 'The environment is certainly the major priority' or similar.

Another useful way to write a balanced conclusion is to use *Provided that* or *As long as* to set a condition on your conclusion. For example:

Overall, it seems that video games can be a useful part of a child's education, provided that the content is monitored by parents and teachers.

To sum up, it appears that tourism is a benefit to less developed countries, as long as some of the profits are reinvested in the local infrastructure.

In any conclusion to a Task 2 essay, try to have a balanced conclusion. The simplest way to do this is to use *one among a range of/as long as/provided that.*

Practice Task

Some people feel that public money should not be spent on cultural amenities such as museums, theatres and art festivals. How important do you think these things are to society as a whole? Are there any areas which are more important for the government to fund?

Remember to practise the points we have studies about complex sentences, academic phrases and having a balanced conclusion.

BOOK FIVE
TASK 2 ESSAY PLANNING

Book Five: Task 2 Essay Planning

Introduction to Book Five

It's quite common to hear an IELTS examiner say about a Task 2 essay, 'This candidate's English is pretty good, they could get Band 7.5 at least . . . but the essay doesn't have a plan. What a shame!' And that candidate gets a Band 6, for example, because their essay is disorganized and confusing.

The fact is that IELTS Academic Writing Task 2 can be challenging even for native speakers of English, and everyone will benefit from making a short plan before starting to write. The plan takes only five minutes to create, but it can make the difference between getting the band score you need and missing it completely.

In this book, we show you fifteen new essays, all written to Band 9 standard, together with the essay plan which the writer created first. There are also examiner's notes which show you how the examiner will judge your essay in terms of its structure, content, style and language.

Remember, your essay plan is purely for you to use; at the end of the test, any plans or notes that you make are collected and destroyed by the examiners. But the plan will help you write the best essay possible, and the examiner will always notice that you have planned carefully. If you need a dictionary while reading this book, we recommend the free *Cambridge Dictionaries Online* from Cambridge University Press.

Don't just trust to luck in your IELTS exam – it's too important. The key is expert advice!

Jessica Alperne & Peter Swires
Cambridge IELTS Consultants
cambridgeielts@outlook.com

Frequently Asked Questions About IELTS Essay Planning

Why do I need to make a plan before writing in Task 2?

It's essential in Task 2 to show the examiner that you have analysed the Task, understood the type of essay needed, and that your ideas are clear and logical. Making an essay plan will help you to do this, and also to organise your ideas, examples and evidence for the main body.

How long should I spend making this plan?

Five minutes maximum is the best use of time. Remember the ideal time management in Task 2:

5 minutes (maximum) planning
30 minutes writing
5 minutes (minimum) checking for any mistakes

How do I make the plan?

You will have spare paper on your exam desk. Using your pen, circle the key words on the Task and make a note of the type of task this is, remembering our overview of the different types.

Ask yourself: is this an Ideas or an Opinion type task? Which type of Ideas or Opinion task is it? Do I understand the topic and the instruction itself?

When this is clear, make some short notes under the following headings:

Task Type
Intro
Main Body
(+ Concession if this is an Opinion>Personal viewpoint Task ONLY)
Conclusion (for Opinion tasks) or **Summary** (for Ideas tasks)

Under '**Intro**' note any background information you can use in the introduction; make a note to show the examiner that you understand the task type. For an Opinion>Personal viewpoint task ONLY, this means giving your opinion in the introduction.

Under '**Main Body**' note two or three ideas for each aspect of the argument, with any examples or evidence you can think of. For example, in an Opinion>Discussion task, note two or three ideas on each side of the discussion; in an Ideas>problems/solutions Task, note two or three problems, then two or three solutions.

You don't need to use more than three ideas for each aspect, but you must have at least two!

Under '**Conclusion**,' note your opinion (in Opinion Tasks) or quickly sum up your main body ideas (in Ideas Tasks.)

Remember, this plan will not be seen by anyone except you, so it doesn't need to be written neatly or in complete sentences. A possible example of a typical plan is:

Example Task

Some commentators feel that grandparents should live together with their children and grandchildren, while others say that older people should be encouraged to live independently.

Consider the possible arguments on both sides of this debate, and reach your own conclusion.

Student's Plan

Essay type: Opinion>Discussion

Intro: traditional vs affordable debate

For living with family:

1 Traditional: More emotional support, eg in bereavement
2 More security (against crime and accidents)
3 Cheaper, may increase quality of life

For living independently:

1 Increases self-reliance and independence, self-esteem
2 Family may not have space or time
3 Allows grandparents to have families visit them, enjoyment

Conclusion: Better to live alone, provided that health/finances allow this

This is a classic Task 2 plan, helping the candidate to think of ideas and organise evidence and examples. The complete essay is shown in our 'Example Task 1' on the next pages in this book. You see that the plan is written in simple English, in short notes and incomplete sentences, for speed.

A model essay for this task and plan is in the next section in this book.

How do I use the plan while I'm writing?

You should look quickly at the plan before you start each paragraph, to remind you of the points for each section. It would be almost impossible to remember all the ideas and examples unless you check the plan. As you write the essay, you will need to change the simple words in your plan for more advanced words (eg *cheaper>less costly* or *better>stronger argument*.)

To ensure that you are on track, remember to count the number of words you have written after you finish each paragraph, and also check the time frequently.

In this book, we have noted the number of words after each essay so that you can see the word count, but in the real exam you don't need to do this.

Modules with Tasks, Essay Plans, Band 9 Model Essays and Examiner's Notes

Module 1

Example Task

Some commentators feel that grandparents should live together with their children and grandchildren, while others say that elderly people should be encouraged to live independently.

Consider the possible arguments on both sides of this debate, and reach your own conclusion.

Explanation of the Task

This is an Opinion > Discussion type Task, requiring you to discuss both sides of a topic and then give your view. You should introduce the topic, make it clear that this will be a Discussion essay, and then give two or three ideas to support each side in the debate. You should give your own opinion in the conclusion.

Remember that the instruction *'Consider the possible arguments on both sides of this debate, and reach your own conclusion'* may be expressed in many different ways in the IELTS test, but the principle for this Task type will be the same.

Student's Plan

Essay type: Opinion>Discussion

Intro: traditional vs affordable debate

For living with family:

1 Traditional: More emotional support, e.g. in bereavement
2 More security (against crime and accidents)
3 Cheaper, may increase quality of life

For living independently:

1 Increases self-reliance and independence, self-esteem
2 Family may not have space or time

3 Allows grandparents to have families visiting them, enjoyment

<u>Conclusion</u>: Better to live alone, provided that health/finances allow this

Band 9 Model Essay

The issue of whether grandparents should live with their extended families is partly a question of the traditions in different cultures or nationalities. However, the question of affordability also plays an increasing part, and so this debate is rather complex, as we shall see.

On the one hand, those who support the idea of grandparents living with their children point to the higher level of emotional support which all family members may receive in such situations, for example in times of crisis such as bereavement. Furthermore, it is also true that personal security may be increased, offering protection against such problems as accidents or even robbery. Finally, it seems that extended family life will also be considerably less costly, for instance with lower food and utility bills, meaning that enjoyment of life may be higher.

By contrast, supporters of grandparents living independently often state that elderly people should be encouraged to be as self-reliant as possible, as this boosts their self-esteem and may guard against mental decline in old age. They also say, with some merit, that many younger families these days do not have the housing space, or indeed the spare time, which is necessary to care properly for older members. As a last point, it is also true that many grandparents prefer to see their grandchildren on a less frequent basis (as opposed to every day), making these visits more special and cherished for all concerned.

Overall, it appears to me that the stronger argument is in favour of grandparents living independently, with all the advantages of self-reliance and separate space. This is provided that their health and finances allow them to continue living separately, without risk or the fear of isolation.

(282 words)

Examiner's notes

This is a clearly structured and logical Opinion > Discussion essay, which would certainly achieve Band 9. The candidate clarifies at the start that the essay will 'debate' the discussion, and the main body emphasises the two opposing views with helpful linking phrases ('On the one hand . . . By contrast . . .') The main body has three clear ideas on each side, and the writer uses a variety of phrases to report the two aspects ('Supporters point to . . . state . . . say, with some merit . .

.') The use of conjunctions to show the transition from one idea to the next inside each paragraph is excellent ('Furthermore . . . Finally . . . They also say . . . As a last point . . .')

The candidate avoids emotion or excessive personalisation by using 'It seems . . . It appears that . . .' which is a strong feature of academic writing. The conclusion is clearly introduced ('Overall . . .) and recaps briefly on the debate, adding a 'proviso' with 'This is provided that . . .' which makes the opinion balanced and more complex.

The language used is formal/academic but also modern (I noted in particular 'bereavement, utility, boost, merit, self-reliance.')

I have the impression of a well-organised candidate, who can use the key elements of academic writing to discuss an issue logically and very clearly.

Module 2

Example Task

'For all children, the ability to play a musical instrument is just as important as the ability to read and write.'

How far do you agree with this suggestion? How important is it for a child to learn to play a musical instrument, in your view?

Explanation of the Task

This is an Opinion > Personal Viewpoint type task. It does not ask you to debate both sides of a topic, but to say how much you agree with an idea. You should introduce the topic and give your opinion in the introduction. The main body should explain your reasons for your view, with two or three supporting ideas. You should mention the opposing view briefly, and then reject it (this is called the 'concession.') The conclusion should state your opinion again and summarise some of the main supporting ideas.

Student's Plan

Essay type: Opinion>Personal Viewpoint

Intro: I don't agree for all children

Main Body:

1 Not all children are musically talented
2 Literacy is a guarantee of education and progress; music is not (eg few professional musicians)
3 Music should be one of a range of optional activities (eg with sport, hobbies, reading)

Concession: For some (a few) children music is essential, but not all

Conclusion: Literacy more important than playing music. Music a secondary, optional activity, can be invaluable for some.

Band 9 Model Essay

The question of which skills to prioritise for a child's early education is important for all parents and educators, and music can certainly claim to be a key possibility when deciding which abilities to teach. However, I feel that playing music is actually less important than basic literacy, and I will explain the reasons here.

Firstly, it seems simplistic to say that music is paramount 'for all children.' Certainly, there are some children who are highly talented or have great interest in music, and, when we think of childhood prodigies such as Beethoven or Yehudi Menuhin, we see how this talent can be brought out. However, such talents are rare, and even the enjoyment and cultural values to be gained from learning music cannot genuinely be compared to the benefits of becoming literate. Secondly, it is a fact that literacy is a guarantee of academic progress and the absorption of information, while playing music does not offer this security. For example, it would be unimaginable to transmit scientific or mathematical information to children via the medium of music. Finally, it is surely wiser to regard music as one of a wide range of secondary skills, ranking below literacy and sitting alongside sports, hobbies, foreign languages and other important but less essential activities.

Of course, those who say that highly talented children must be allowed to develop their talents are quite correct; it is equally true, though, that few children seem to possess musical ability to the extent that it should be prioritised so highly for all pupils.

In conclusion, I would not wish to underestimate the potential benefits of learning to play music for a minority of children, and it should certainly be available as an option. However, if we think of all children in a given community, literacy appears to be a far stronger pathway to progress and independence.

(309 words)

Examiner's notes

This candidate has produced a Band 9 essay with clear structure, logical ideas and a strong command of Academic English. The introduction introduces some general background about the topic and makes it clear that the essay will be the appropriate Opinion>Personal viewpoint type.

The main body is largely given to an explanation of the candidate's reasons for thinking this, which are sequenced well with 'Firstly/secondly/finally.' In this section, the writer avoids using 'I' and uses impersonal structures instead ('it seems . . . when we think of . . . it is a fact that . . . it is surely') which we would expect in Academic writing in English. There is a short 'concession' paragraph that mentions the opposing view and then counters it with a logical objection.

The language throughout is academic in style but is never too formal or complicated. For instance, the part which reads . . .

'Secondly, it is a fact that literacy is a guarantee of academic progress and the absorption of information, while playing music does not offer this security. For example, it would be unimaginable to transmit scientific or mathematical information to children via the medium of music.'

. . . is an excellent demonstration of complex sentences (i.e. sentences with several ideas) written in a clear way which is similar to academic writing or advanced journalism which one might read in the media.

The two musical geniuses given as examples are sufficiently well-known to be relevant (this is something which can cause problems when candidates reference people whom they know about but who are not widely known to the public.)

The conclusion is effective in summarising the main ideas and recapping on the writer's opinion.

As an examiner, I start reading an IELTS essay by wanting to give the highest possible mark, and nothing here would stop me from giving a Band 9 here.

Module 3

Example Task

*In many countries, truancy * is a worrying problem for both parents and educators. What are the causes of truancy, and what may be the effects on the child and the wider community?*

(truancy = the situation when a child pretends to go to school but in fact goes somewhere else, for example to play unsupervised. The verb is 'to play truant from school.')*

Explanation of the Task

This is an Ideas > Causes/Effects type Task. It does not ask you to say if truancy is a good or bad thing, but it asks you to think of ideas about why truancy happens and the impact on children and the community. You should introduce the topic briefly, then suggest two or three causes, plus two or three effects, and then summarise in the conclusion without expressing a personal view.

Sometimes, a Task will give you a definition of a word or phrase; make sure you read this carefully and use the words accurately in the essay, because the meaning might be different from what you initially think.

Student's Plan

Type: ideas>causes/effects (effects on child & community)

Intro: this is cause/effect essay

Possible causes:
1 Boredom with school, dull lessons
2 Peer pressure, other children do it

Possible effects:
1 Lack of progress, & career problems (child)
2 Tempted into crime (child)
3 Petty crime eg vandalism, litter, anti-social behaviour (community)

Summary: Causes can be academic & from peers; effects are to do with crime & behaviour

Band 9 Model Essay

Truancy is an activity which some children regard as amusing or even exciting, but which can have serious impacts on their future and on society as a whole. I can identify two main causes, and three broad effects, which we will describe now.

Perhaps the main cause is a sense of boredom or frustration with school itself, for instance with the content, pace or organisation of the lessons. This can be seen in the way that pupils often avoid certain lessons but not others, suggesting that specific subjects or teachers are the personal grievance. Another factor may frequently be peer pressure, meaning that pupils feel obliged to play truant because some of their peers or friends are doing this. We can see that the child's desire to be popular among a peer group may be higher than the motivation to study and progress.

Turning to possible effects, the tendency to underperform academically is probably the most serious impact on a pupil's life, leading to poor exam results and weak career progression in later life. Another effect may be the temptation to participate in petty crime or antisocial behaviour while the child is unsupervised, potentially opening a pathway into more serious crimes later on. For example, a child who commits vandalism may progress to theft and robbery, a trend we see in some major South American cities such as Rio or Buenos Aires. This issue of crime is probably the third major effect, and one that impacts on the community as a whole. For instance, children playing truant may cause damage, drop litter, intimidate elderly people and commit other acts which spread a sense of instability and anxiety, even though the financial impact is low.

To sum up, the causes of truancy generally relate to lack of challenge or peer pressures, while the effects are seen in individual under-achievement and in minor crime against the community as a whole.

(315 words)

<u>Examiner's notes</u>

This candidate has produced a logical and clear to read essay which answers the Cause>Effect Task to a Band 9 standard. The introduction tells me that she has identified the essay type, and advises me to expect to read about two causes and three effects.

The main body uses tentative language effectively ('<u>Perhaps</u> the main cause . . . Another factor <u>may</u> frequently be . . . <u>may</u> be higher than . . .' etc) which adds a sense of objectivity. The second paragraph is introduced clearly ('Turning to . . .') and the ideas are separated helpfully ('Another effect . . . the third major effect . . .') showing that the 'three effects' described in the introduction are being explained. The examples given are rather simple, but they certainly illustrate the main ideas in a concise way.

The vocabulary shows a good command of advanced material (eg 'sense of boredom' 'tendency to underperform' 'participate in' 'commit acts') and the impression is that the candidate has read a lot of general commentary in the press or media to help develop this.

The conclusion summarises the main ideas, and expresses them without repeating directly from the main body (eg 'boredom>lack of challenge' 'underperform>under-achievement' 'petty crime>minor crime') which shows a wide range of active vocabulary.

Module 4

Example Task

Many people today are worried about the large quantities of waste produced by ordinary households. What problems are caused by household waste, and what solutions may be possible in both the short and the long term?

Explanation of the Task

This is an Ideas > Problems/solutions type Task. It is not asking for your opinion, but for you to propose some ideas on this topic. You should introduce the topic and essay, and describe two or three problems, then two or three solutions, and then summarise. Note that the task asks for 'both the short and the long term' solutions, so you must mention both of these. Also, the topic is only about household (= domestic) waste, not industrial waste; remember to check these smaller points in the instructions, because in the exam it can be easy to miss them!

Student's Plan

Type: Ideas>problems/solutions

Intro: Background: an increasing problem (domestic waste)

Problems
1 Processing & disposal, eg landfill, recycling
2 Cost of recycling/safe disposal is high (taxes etc)

Solutions
1 Short-term: More funds for recycling, increase use of recycled material
2 Long-term: More education/incentives/penalties to change behaviour

Summary:
Problems = environmental & cost; solutions = short & long term

Band 9 Model Essay

It is inevitable that modern households will produce some waste, but the increasing volumes of refuse over recent years present a challenge for us all. There seem to be two main problems stemming from this situation, and also two steps we could take to address it fully.

Possible the major problem is the huge question of how to collect, process and dispose of this material. Household waste comprises elements ranging from foodstuffs to metal, paper and plastics, and local authorities sometimes struggle to handle such a diverse mix of material. The historical solution has been incineration or landfill, but the problems of pollution and long-term ground contamination which arise have led to widespread efforts to recycle at least some of the waste. This leads us to the second concern, which is the high cost of disposing of refuse in an ecologically sound manner. We would all wish as much as possible of our rubbish to be recycled (for example by paper pulping or reusing plastics) but the expense involved must be met by higher taxes and charges for households.

Regarding possible solutions, probably the most immediate short-term solution would be to divert far more government funds into waste processing and recycling facilities at a local level. This would reduce the environmental impact of the waste by reducing pollution, and also lower our demand for raw materials, as more recycled products would consequently be produced. A further, longer-term solution might be to raise the level of public understanding for the need to consume less material in households, especially in terms of packaging and wasted food. A campaign of education along these lines would gradually lessen the volume of waste, especially if reinforced by incentives for consuming less and penalties for excessive waste, as we see being trialled in the UK at present.

Overall, the main problems are both environmental and financial. The possible solutions involve more immediate investment in facilities, and also encouraging long-term changes in household behaviour.

(326 words)

Examiner's notes

This is a logical and well-organised Band 9 essay, with strong academic style and very effective advanced vocabulary. The introduction tells me clearly that the candidate has considered both the topic and the task, and has prepared a problem/solution main body.

The 'problems' paragraph gives examples in an effective way ('ranging from . . . to') and uses complex sentences which present a variety of ideas (in particular the sentence 'The historical solution . . . some of the waste' which contains three stages of ideas in a logical sequence.) Signposting is excellent ('This leads us to . . . Regarding possible . . .')

The 'solutions' paragraph offers practical ideas without excessive technical detail, and uses tentative language ('would . . . might be') to show that the candidate is discussing *possible* remedies rather than presenting a complete solution. The candidate emphasises that she is presenting short and long term solutions. The level of vocabulary is excellent, both in terms of academic English (eg 'stemming from . . . comprises . . . divert funds . . . reinforced by incentives') and topic-specific language (eg 'incineration . . . ecologically sound . . . paper pulping . . . environmental impact.') We don't expect candidates to know scientific or very specialised words, but this vocabulary is used widely on this topic in the general media.

The summary is rather brief, but it covers the main ideas well, and at 326 words I would not want the essay to be much longer.

Module 5

Example Task

'People who do not use social media networks will always fall behind in career development opportunities.'

To what extent do you feel that this is an accurate and important prediction?

(Social media networks = messaging and information exchange systems such as Facebook and Twitter.)

Explanation of the Task

This is an Opinion > personal viewpoint type task (like Example Task number 2 in this book.) Remember that this type is different from the Opinion>Discussion type; here, give you opinion in the introduction, and use the main body to explain your reasons. Have a short 'concession' paragraph, and then summarise your opinion and reasons very briefly in the conclusion.

Remember not to use excessive detail in your evidence and examples! You probably have a lot of information about a topic such as social media, but your evidence needs to be accessible to a general reader.

Student's Plan

Essay type: Opinion>Personal viewpoint

Introduction: Background; I don't agree with 'always' in the statement

Main body reasons;

1 Qualifications etc are more important (eg doctors)

2 Interpersonal skills are more powerful, (eg negotiation)

3 Social media has risks (eg pics/comments), some people minimise SM because of this

Concession: True that social media is good for networking; but this is *after* success, not before

Conclusion: Recap on qualifications/personal skills, and the concession

Band 9 Model Essay

Social media plays an increasingly pivotal role in our lives, and an ability to use these systems is certainly an advantage both socially and professionally. However, it seems rather excessive to say that ignorance of these matters will 'always' restrict people's careers, and I will explain why.

Firstly, career progression relies on a whole range of factors, not only on the use of social media. For example, a professional person will have a range of qualifications, ranging from academic exams to vocational certificates and membership of professional bodies. We see this in the way that successful doctors take increasingly specialised qualifications and join specific institutes to develop their skills. Here, social media may be a communication tool, but is surely not the driving force behind success. Secondly, career development relies greatly on interpersonal skills such as presentation methods, persuasiveness and negotiation, all of which are used in face-to-face situations rather than remotely. Finally, we should remember the dangers of social media and the risk of actually hindering one's career, for instance by accidentally distributing awkward photos or comments which can be an embarrassment personally and professionally. Indeed, many professionals in fact minimise their use of these media because of this risk.

Admittedly, it is true that social media presents great opportunities for making contacts and networking, for example by building a following or exchanging updates on a particular topic. However, this tends to happen when a person is already qualified and respected in their field, rather than being a cause of success.

In conclusion, it appears that skilful use of these media can play a useful role in career progression, despite the possible risks. Nevertheless, the fundamental qualifications and personal skills which drive a career will ensure that those who are not enthusiastic users will still progress as they wish.

(302 words)

Examiner's notes

This is an impressive Band 9 essay: clear for me to read, with suitable ideas and evidence.

The intro helps me to anticipate what will be in the main body ('I will explain why') and, by focussing on the key word 'always,' it shows that the candidate has analysed the task carefully. This is a strong start.

The main body has strong linking between ideas ('Firstly . . . Secondly . . . Finally') and the evidence is presented with a range of structures ('For example . . . such as . . . for instance . . . ranging from/to . . . we see this in the way . . .') which add variety. The concession is clearly introduced ('Admittedly') and the opposing view is rejected in a logical way. The conclusion is balanced ('Nevertheless') and is an effective recap of the main ideas.

The academic style is very effective, with a number of complex sentences (sentences with two or more ideas) especially in main body and conclusion. Some of the vocab is quite simple (eg 'face-to-face') but this fits the argument well; elsewhere, the vocabulary shows a very advanced grasp, especially words such as 'pivotal, vocational, to hinder, fundamental.'

One point I would like to emphasise is the nature of the ideas in this essay. The candidate's reasons for his opinion are based on quite simple reasons, which he explains with clear examples. As an examiner, I like to see such simple, clearly-explained reasons which allow the candidate to demonstrate his skills of organisation and Academic English style.

Module 6

Example Task

'Knowing how to make a group presentation is the most important skill for anyone in the world of work today.'

How important are presentation and public speaking skills, compared to various other work skills? Which skill is the most important ability for most people these days?

Explanation of the Task

This is an Ideas > Evaluate type essay, which is the least common type in the IELTS writing test. The Task is not asking for an opinion about presentation skills in isolation, but is asking you to compare the importance of this skill to various other skills, and to decide which is the most important.

You should introduce the topic and give an outline of your decision in the introduction, then use the main body to show your 'ranking' of what is important. You can simply do this by saying 'The most important is . . . the second most important is . . .' and so on. Three ideas are enough for the main body (ie a 'ranking' of three skills, in this example) with your reasons/evidence for deciding on this ranking.

The summary should briefly recap on the ranking and your reasons.

Student's Plan

Essay Type: Ideas>Evaluate

Introduction: A range of skills needed; 2 others more important than presentational

Main Body:

1 (Most important) Time management/prioritising, eg for medicine, conferences less important

2 (2nd important) Team management, public & private sector, social media replaces public speaking

3 Presentation skills are 3rd most important today, work is changing

Conclusion: Don't neglect speaking skills, but this is number 3 in workplace now

Band 9 Model Essay

Success at work these days requires a wide range of skills, of which presentational ability is certainly among the most important. However, there are two other skills which appear to be more useful, which we will evaluate now.

Possibly the key skill in professional life today is in fact the ability to handle a high workload, including the methods of prioritising tasks and managing one's time in an effective way. In most professions, this skill has grown in importance hugely over recent years, while the need for public speaking has probably remained static. For example, in the medical field, doctors attend increasingly fewer conferences and seminars, because these events are perceived as time-consuming and less productive than they used to be due to the ease of exchanging information remotely.

The second most important skill is probably the capacity to manage teams of people, including the techniques of setting and monitoring team objectives. This ability is fundamental to modern organisations in both business and the public sector, and success in this area virtually guarantees a person professional advancement, even if their public speaking skills are less developed. We see this in the way in which finance or consumer goods companies promote effective team managers, but rarely require them to address large groups of people. The same trend can be seen in the civil administration and public services, where public speaking has to some extent been replaced by use of social media.

For these reasons, I would evaluate presentation skills as a tertiary skill, which is important but increasingly less useful than in the past, due to the radical changes in the way we work together and communicate with each other professionally.

Overall, it is true that professional people should not neglect or underestimate the usefulness of speaking skills. However, the skills of workload management and team direction appear to be more relevant and decisive in today's rapidly evolving workplace.

Examiner's notes

'Evaluate' type essays can be difficult to write effectively, because the candidate sometimes tries to write about how 'good or bad' something is, rather than 'where in the ranking' it is. This essay clarifies in its introduction that the writer is going to evaluate and present a ranking of importance, leading us neatly into the main body.

The reasons given for placing the 'time management' and 'team management' skills above 'presentation' skills are explained with relevant examples which are persuasive without requiring specialised knowledge. Each of these skills is compared to 'presentation' skills, and logical reasons are given with evidence for deciding that they are more important. The candidate uses a very effective mix of tentative language (eg 'Possibly the key skill . . . probably remained static . . . The second most important skill is probably . . .) and also persuasive descriptions (eg 'events are perceived' 'fundamental' 'virtually guarantees' 'We see this in the way . . .') This combination of tentative, impersonal phrases and more persuasive phrases is something I reward with a high band score.

The language shows a strong level of advanced, Academic English, although it is noticeable that all the language is today widely used in the press and media. For instance, 'static' 'perceived as' 'fundamental' 'monitor objectives' 'tertiary' 'radical changes' 'rapidly evolving.' These are all common words when topics are discussed in a professional way.

Module 7

Example Task

Some people feel that the exploration of space justifies a large amount of government and private investment. Other people think that this field is of increasingly low relevance, and should not be a priority.

Debate both sides of this discussion, and explain your own view. How important is it for us to explore space at the moment?

Explanation of the Task

This is another Opinion > Discussion type Task. The introduction should make it clear that you understand the Task type, by saying 'There are arguments on both sides . . . as we will see' or similar. Explain two or three ideas on each side of the debate, and give your opinion in the conclusion.

Remember to decide your opinion when you are making your plan. The second main body paragraph should connect with the opinion in the conclusion, as you see in this model essay.

Student's Plan

Essay Type: Opinion>Discussion

Intro: Background; discussion essay intro

For exploration:
1 Technical progress (eg plastics)
2 Helps solve issues, eg biology (eg ISS genetics research)

Against exploration
1 High cost; doesn't benefit everyone; most advances are not due to space
2 Academic pursuit; funding today doesn't allow it; we can solve problems without it (eg wildlife etc)

Conclusion: Against space research; too costly now; space will always be there

Band 9 Model Essay

Space exploration is a subject which provokes great emotions as well as scientific interest, and at times the two become somewhat blurred. There are strong arguments on both sides of the debate about whether to continue space travel, which we will discuss here.

On the one hand, those who urge the continued exploration of space say that this field has given us substantial technical advances over the past fifty years, ranging from better plastics and alloys to a greater understanding of flight and gravity. Furthermore, they claim that further investigations will help to solve some of mankind's most pressing issues, such as lack of food and environmental damage, because the study of (for example) biology and chemistry can be carried out more radically in space. Recent experiments on the International Space Station in the field of genetics certainly seem to support this view.

Conversely, however, people who oppose more funding for space research point to the extremely high costs involved, compared to the practical benefits which are gained for almost all members of the human race. For example, these opponents state that all the major developments in terms of medicine, genetics, materials and mechanics have actually been as a result of terrestrial science and experiments, rather than stemming from space exploration. Moreover, they feel that space investigation is largely an academic pursuit, fascinating though it is, and that at a time of austerity our funding should be directed to more practical programmes to help people. It is indeed true that addressing some major human challenges such as pollution control, protection of wildlife and greater political stability would not require any involvement at all by space scientists.

Overall, I feel that the opponents of high funding for space have the stronger argument at present. It seems that the enormous sums involved could be used more practically to deal with some of our most immediate problems. After all, space will always be there to explore, when funding and other problems make its research more affordable for us as a species.

(338 words)

Examiner's notes

This candidate has achieved Band 9 by reporting the ideas on both sides of the discussion in an objective, academic way, with strong use of examples. The intro has an interesting background comment, and confirms that this is a 'Discussion' type essay.

In the main body, the candidate uses 'reporting' language very effectively (eg 'those who urge . . . they claim . . .those who oppose . . . these opponents . . .') and also adds some approval of the evidence used in the argument by saying,

'Recent experiments . . . certainly seem to support this view . . . It is indeed true that . . .' This combination of impersonal style and validating the evidence makes the essay seem authoritative.

The language has some strong examples of academic collocations (= words which are traditionally used together):

'Somewhat blurred . . . practical benefits . . . greater understanding . . . academic pursuit . . . the enormous sums involved.'

The conclusion is quite long, but it is balanced and provides a logical support for the writer's opinion. I am glad that the essay stopped at that point, because 338 words is close to the maximum that I would wish to read. The best essays that I see tend to be around 300 to 320 words.

Module 8

Example Task

Some employers are willing to give their workers a certain amount of unpaid sabbatical time, believing this will benefit the individual and the organisation. Other employers see no merit in this arrangement and discourage it.*

Consider the possible arguments for and against unpaid sabbatical leave, and reach a viewpoint of your own.

(unpaid sabbatical time or leave = extended, unpaid time off work, in which an employee can follow personal interests or studies, and then return to work)*

Explanation of the Task

This is another Opinion>Discussion task, the most common type in the writing test.

Note the keywords 'unpaid leave' and 'employers,' which are inviting you to consider the cost aspect to a business in your answer, and also 'the individual and the organisation' which is telling you to think about both these perspectives.

Student's Plan

Essay type: Opinion>Discussion

Intro: Background; fashionable idea; discussion intro

For unpaid leave:
1 Motivating; workers are refreshed
2 Low cost; can help with restructures etc

Against it
1 Disruption; people need to be replaced
2 Workers lose interest/go to competitors
3 More suited to academic work, research etc

Conclusion: Problems outweigh advantages; ok for individuals, but difficult for company and colleagues

Band 9 Model Essay

The idea of offering employees sabbatical time has become quite fashionable recently, with some major companies believing it has great benefits. However, there is also substantial opposition to the concept, and we will discuss the two views now.

Those employers who support unpaid sabbaticals often highlight the motivating effect which such leave can have on an employee. They feel that, at a time when people are under pressure, a certain amount of extended leave can allow someone to return to work feeling refreshed and more committed to the company. A second point in favour is that such leave does not cost the company anything, as the employee stops drawing a salary. Indeed, it seems that such breaks might actually save money, as departments can be downsized without the need for redundancies or compensation.

On the other hand, many other employers feel that this practice has a disruptive effect which outweighs its possible benefit to the individual. For example, if employees have a certain skill or responsibility, they must be replaced by someone who is similarly qualified, probably involving a cost in training or hiring a new worker. Companies are also reluctant to allow skilled employees to drift away from their business, fearing, with some justification, that the person might lose interest or even go to work for a competitor. Finally, some employers feel that the whole idea of sabbaticals is more suited to an academic context such as universities or research institutes, where the employee will be working on personal interests which coincide with their field of study, which is rarely the case among corporate employees.

To sum up, it seems true that the problems caused by unpaid sabbaticals do indeed outweigh the potential advantages. Although the individual employee may be refreshed, the disruption and costs caused by this absence are unreasonable for the company and for the colleagues left behind at work.

(312 words)

Examiner's notes

This is a topic where candidates sometimes struggle to find suitable ideas, but this candidate has obviously planned her ideas carefully, which is very noticeable.

The simple introduction guides the reader into the 'Discussion' main body. The ideas are explained helpfully, with strong use of examples which use some good topic-specific vocabulary ('downsize, redundancies, competitor, corporate.') Signposting is very effective, with each new idea being introduced with a conjunction, and the reporting of the views on each side is done in an impersonal way that does not commit the writer to a conclusion until the final paragraph. This is important in a task which asks us to 'consider arguments . . . and *reach* a viewpoint.'

The conclusion itself returns to the task instruction of 'the individual and the organisation' by weighing the two perspectives against each other. This shows me that the candidate has planned the conclusion and has been building towards it.

Module 9

Example Task

Light pollution (excessive light during night time) is a form of pollution that distresses many people, especially in modern cities. What are the causes of light pollution, and what solutions can you suggest for governments and businesses to take?

Explanation of the Task

This is an Ideas>Mixed>Causes/solutions type Task.

The most common 'Ideas' types are Cause/effect and Problem/solution, but sometimes the Task may mix the elements to give Causes/solutions or Problems/effects. You need to check the instructions carefully to make sure if this is the case in your test. If this happens, you need to make clear in the introduction that you have understood this, and then describe two or three ideas for each paragraph in the main body. The summary should briefly recap on the main ideas.

Remember that in Ideas type tasks, you should not give a personal opinion. You should report on the situation as it exists in the wider society as a whole.

Important keywords in this Task are 'cities' and 'governments and businesses'; see in our example how the candidate has planned to address these points.

Student's Plan

Essay type: Ideas>Mixed>Causes/solutions (govts & business)

Intro: Background (topical in cities); 3 causes and 2 solutions

Causes (in cities):
1 Advertising signs eg Moscow, Tokyo
2 Street lamps/security lights (against accidents/crime)
3 Vehicle lights

Solutions:
1 Banning lights wouldn't work; better to have light insulation for homes (by governments)
2 Voluntary 'dark day' each week to reduce advertising lighting (by businesses)

Summary: Causes are advertising & public lighting; solutions are insulation & voluntary reductions

Band 9 Model Essay

As more of us live in cities, the question of light pollution is becoming increasingly topical and important to address. There seem to be three main causes, and also two key solutions which we could take to lessen the problem.

The main cause is almost certainly the use of lighting for advertising in public spaces. For example, if we look at cities such as Tokyo or Moscow, almost all available surfaces are fitted with some form of light, often for announcements or commercial use. This huge expansion in illuminated advertising is partly a result of competitive pressures, and also due to the power of such advertising, with flashing lights, video and pictures. A secondary cause is the large number or street lamps and security lights used in cities, which are intended to reduce accidents and crime by removing shadow areas at night. Finally, high levels of night-time traffic also produce light pollution, as drivers use headlamps which shine into windows and gardens after dark.

Turning to possible remedies, it might be tempting for governments to ban or regulate electric advertising billboards, but in many cases (for example in New York or London) these signs are now a local symbol. It would also be difficult to reduce security and traffic lights, because these are needed to keep residents and travellers safe. I would rather see a government-backed programme of light protection for private homes, involving better insulation against outside light after dark. This would allow residents to rest in their homes without being disturbed by the lights in the streets outside. Additionally, a voluntary 'dark day' once per week, supported by business advertisers, in which all commercial lighting is reduced, would allow residents to experience a more natural level of darkness without jeopardizing their safety.

In summary, advertising and public lighting are the main factors behind this problem. Better light insulation, and occasional voluntary reductions in commercial lighting, would greatly help the residents to live more in peace with a brightly illuminated environment.

(332 words)

Examiner's notes

A 'Mixed' essay type requires the candidate to be flexible and pay great attention to the instructions to ensure that the Task is answered. This candidate has planned carefully, and achieves a Band 9 by organising clear ideas and explaining them effectively.

The introduction gives some background to the topic and informs me that there will be three causes and two solutions in the main body. The first cause is explained on two levels (advertising>commercial pressures) which suggests that the writer has planned the argument well. Signposting is very clear ('A secondary cause . . . Finally . . . Turning to possible remedies etc.') The 'solutions' paragraph is quite sophisticated because it rejects one possible solution in favour of another one ('I would rather see a . . .') with a logical rationale for this.

The benefits of the proposed solutions are explained ('This would allow . . .') which is something that candidates often omit to do. The summary recaps on the main ideas of the main body without repeating exactly the same language.

The English used is very natural, with some effective collocations ('competitive pressures' 'business advertisers' 'jeopardize safety') and advanced language for discussing solutions ('ban or regulate' 'government-backed programme' 'voluntary reductions.')

Module 10

Example Task

The practice of illegal hunting of wild animals continues to cause concern in many countries, particularly developing countries.

What are the causes of such hunting? What are the effects on the animals, and on the wider human society in these countries and beyond?

Explanation of the Task

This is an Ideas > Causes/effects type Task. You should introduce the topic, describe two or three causes, then two or three effects, and then summarise briefly in the final paragraph. 'Animals' and 'wider human society' are important key words in the 'effects' part here.

Remember to avoid emotion or dramatic language, even if the topic is something you care about a lot.

Student's Plan

Essay Type: Ideas>Causes/effects (on animals & society)

Intro: Introduce topic & causes/effects

Causes:
1 Profit eg ivory, medical cures
2 Food; instability, war

Effects:
1 Extinction, disruption to food chain
2 Loss of heritage, eg Siberian tigers

Summary: Sum up the 4 main body ideas

Band 9 Model Essay

Poaching is a phenomenon with a variety of causes, both commercial and cultural. The effects can be extremely serious for animals and the community, as we will discuss now.

Possibly the most common cause of people turning to poaching is the profit which can be made from animal materials. We see this in the high prices attached to illegal ivory, furs and hides, which are highly sought after by a small but wealthy group of unscrupulous global collectors. In turn, these prices may be the result of novelty or rarity value, or connected to imaginary medicinal properties, for example in the illegal trade for bear and gorilla body parts. A secondary cause is the more basic pressure of hunting for food, which forces some local people to kill animals purely for meat. The roots of this tend to be in localised famine or drought, or in political instability which disrupts the food supply, as we see in central Africa currently.

Turning to the effects of poaching, the most serious is the threat of extinction posed to species which are already rare or endangered because of habitat loss or other environmental factors. The resulting consequences of extinction may include damage to the food chain and the ecosphere, in addition, of course, to the loss of a precious form of life. A further effect is the further erosion of a country's natural heritage, which comprises its animals, landscape and natural resources, all of which may be under pressure already. Few could doubt, for example, that Siberia would be vastly poorer without its few remaining Siberian tigers.

Overall, the factors behind poaching tend to be commercial or connected to regional instability. The effects may include final extinction, with the damage to ecosystems and loss of heritage that this involves.

Examiner's notes

This Band 9 essay shows a clear argument and very strong language for describing cause and effect. The intro alerts me to the 'commercial and cultural' aspect of the causes, and these are explained in the first main body paragraph. The candidate shows that she can explain the underlying causes of a situation ('In turn, these prices may be the result of . . . 'The roots of this tend to be . . .') with relevant evidence about ivory/gorillas/central Africa.

The 'effects' paragraph is careful to answer the two elements in the task instruction (animals and society) suggesting to me that the essay is well-planned. The summary paragraph is slightly repetitive of the main body in its vocabulary, but as a recap it is very effective.

The language used displays an excellent range of vocabulary on the specific topic ('poaching, unscrupulous, famine, drought, food chain, natural heritage') and also in general language ('high prices attached to' 'The roots of this' 'The resulting consequences' 'the further erosion' 'Few could doubt, for example, that' in particular.) The IELTS examiners will always be impressed by this combination of advanced/academic phrasing and a certain amount of topic-specific vocabulary.

Module 11

Example Task

'The use of software makes it unnecessary for people to know how to spell words correctly these days.'

Is this a statement that you agree with? To what extent do you agree or disagree?

Explanation of the Task

This is another Opinion > Personal viewpoint task. You should give your opinion in the introduction, and use the main body to justify this with two or three reasons. The 'concession' paragraph should be one or two sentences, and the conclusion should state your opinion again.

Remember that you will improve your score by giving a balanced response (ie not saying 'I totally agree/disagree' but saying 'I partly agree/disagree, because . . .')

Student's Plan

Essay Type: Opinion>Personal viewpoint

Introduction: Spellcheck is useful, but spelling can't be ignored

Main Body:
1 Still need to write manually, eg in exams & notes
2 Spelling is part of language
3 Learning spelling helps mental development (thought, sight, writing etc)

Concession: Software is useful, but a supporting tool

Conclusion: Spelling is essential, for practical & mental reasons

Band 9 Model Essay

Almost everyone uses software to create texts these days, and we all find the 'spellcheck' type features useful. However, it would be unwise for people to completely ignore learning how to spell properly by themselves, for reasons which I will explain here.

Firstly, although we mostly use typing devices, there will always be occasions when we need to write manually or without the support of software. This may be in examinations, which are still mostly handwritten, or when writing letters or notes on paper, or filling in forms. It is essential, for example, that police records or medical notes, which are often quickly completed by hand, are accurately and clearly composed. Secondly, understanding spelling is an integral part of learning a language and the various ways that it can be used. Most educators would agree, for example, that it is impossible to divorce spelling from grammar and syntax as part of a rigorous approach to literacy.

Finally, and perhaps most importantly, the whole process of learning and distinguishing different sounds and spellings is a vital part of a child's mental development, involving the complex relationship between hearing, sight, thought and the writing process itself. To say that this relationship is 'unnecessary' is to neglect some of the most fundamental stages in human development which have driven our progress for the past five thousand years, since the era of hieroglyphics and primitive inscriptions.

It is true that the use of software is an invaluable tool, and may well have a role in the process of teaching children to use computers and improving their work accordingly. However, this means that is a supporting facility, not a replacement for human thought.

In conclusion, I feel that a knowledge of spelling is essential, both for practical reasons and to support the development of a person's mind as they learn to read and write, with all the mental benefits which stem from that. It seems that software is highly unlikely to replace the human mind in this very important respect.

(334 words)

Examiner's notes

This essay would achieve Band 9 due to its very well-organised argument, academic style and range of vocabulary.

In terms of the argument, the candidate gives his view in the intro and then explains his reasons, with clear signposting ('Firstly, secondly, finally.') Simple conjunctions like this are effective as long as the paragraph content is fairly advanced. The concession shows that the writer can consider opposing views and accept that they have some validity, while putting his own judgement on it ('invaluable . . . but a supporting facility.') The conclusion summarises well in new language ('practical reasons' 'mind.')

In terms of style, the writer is very persuasive in using outside opinions as evidence ('Most educators would agree . . .') and in rejecting the Task statement

('To say that this relationship is 'unnecessary' is to neglect . . .') (also showing that he has analysed the Task well.)

The vocabulary includes some very natural and effective collocations which are typical of discussions in the quality media, such as:

an integral part of
impossible to divorce spelling from grammar
a rigorous approach
the complex relationship between . . .
since the era of . . .
all the mental benefits which stem from that.
in this very important respect.

Natural, advanced phrases like this encourage the examiner to award a very high Band score, especially if the structure is also strong.

Module 12

Example Task

The use of phones, tablets and other devices when people are walking in public is causing concern among many commentators. What dangers may arise when people focus on such devices when walking in the street? How could these problems be reduced?

Explanation of the Task

This is an Ideas > Problem/solution type Task. The instructions may sometimes include synonyms for 'problems' such as 'dangers, risks, drawbacks' and synonyms for 'solutions' including 'answers, remedies, ways to solve/reduce.'

Student's Plan

Essay type: Ideas>Problems/solutions
Intro: Devices are universal; 2 problems, 2 solutions

Problems:
1 Accidents, eg people, cars, traffic
2 Anti-social & rude

Solutions:
1 Education about dangers, eg in colleges, advertising
2 put warning systems on phones, like on cars

Summary: Physical & social dangers; education & warning for solutions

Band 9 Model Essay

As hand-held devices become almost universal in our society, the number of accidents related to their use is increasing accordingly, in addition to various social dangers. I will outline two such risks, and also two possible counter-measures we could take.

Firstly, the greatest danger is surely the possibility of people failing to pay attention to their surroundings when they use such items while walking along pavements, public areas and streets. By diverting all their attention (both visual and in most cases mental) onto their device, the users may bump into other people, fall over uneven surfaces or even step into traffic lanes, with potentially fatal results. A number of deaths among teenagers in the UK, for example, is attributable to this cause each year. A second problem must be the rather anti-social nature of people focussing all their thoughts on a device, to the exclusion of others around them, who may need help or guidance as much as basic courtesy. The increasingly impolite atmosphere in many public spaces may well be connected to this phenomenon.

Turning to possible solutions, it would be helpful to see a joint initiative between the authorities and mobile phone producers to raise public awareness of these risks. Such a programme could take many forms, ranging from advertising to dedicated classes in schools and colleges, and could be aimed at both the problem of accidents and the unsociable nature of excessive device usage, which would make it very cost-effective. A further solution may be to install warning mechanisms on these devices, which detect when traffic or obstacles are nearby, so that the user does not walk blindly into danger. Such systems already exist in cars to alert drivers to impending trouble or the need to change direction.

Overall, the dangers in this situation are both physical and social. Potential remedies may involve better education, and also enhanced danger detection along the lines already used successfully in motor vehicles.

(321 words)

Examiner's notes

This candidate has answered the Task in an imaginative way, with organisation which makes the essay clear and persuasive and achieving Band 9. The intro impressed me immediately, with its clear outline of the essay and use of 'counter-measures' as a synonym for 'solutions.'

The 'problems' section proposes physical and social dangers, and both are supported by relevant evidence (although I would have liked to see something a bit more definite as evidence for the 'anti-social' idea.) The candidate uses the 'By + -ing . . . the (subject) may + verb' structure ('By diverting all their attention onto their device, the users may bump into . . .) to explain the physical problem; this is a simple device which works well here.

The 'solutions' section is quite creative (joint initiative and warning system) and the ways of implementing the 'initiative' are clearly explained ('could take many forms, ranging from advertising to dedicated classes . . .') using 'would' and 'could' to show that this is an idea, not a reality. It would be awkward to use 'will' or 'must' in these situations. The writer links between the sentences well using 'such' (eg '. . . these risks. Such a programme' '. . . blindly into danger. Such systems . . .'

The summary uses fresh vocabulary to sum up, which impressed me again.

The language throughout is advanced, and shows a strong grasp of collocations (eg Potentially fatal, anti-social, increasingly impolite, joint initiative, walk blindly, impending trouble.) Phrases such as 'Turning to possible solutions' and 'along the lines already used' add to the very natural tone of the essay.

Module 13

Example Task

Some governments today seek to monitor the general public's electronic communications (in the form of phone calls, texts and emails) saying that this reduces crime. Many people oppose this, however, saying that it erodes individual freedoms.

Discuss the aspects of this debate, and give your own conclusion to the discussion.

Explanation of the Task

This is another Opinion > Discussion type Task. There is quite a lot of information in the instruction; you are not expected to discuss the differences between 'phone calls, texts and emails' but focus on the principle of 'monitoring' and 'reducing crime' versus 'individual freedoms.'

Notice how the candidate's plan connects the 'against monitoring' paragraph to the 'against monitoring' conclusion.

Student's Plan

Essay type: Opinion>Discussion

Intro: background; confirm 'discussion' type essay

Main Body:

Supporting monitoring:
1 Known to reduce crime (eg in USA)
2 'Nothing to hide, nothing to fear' idea

Against monitoring:
1 Breach of liberties (eg would we allow police to search our homes?)
2 Very low conviction rate; better to act on specific information

Conclusion: monitoring does not justify loss of freedom; police need to be more focussed

Band 9 Model Essay

It is admirable that governments seek to reduce criminality, and are prepared to use modern methods to achieve this. However, the arguments on both sides of this particular discussion (about monitoring private electronic correspondence) are by no means straightforward, as we shall see now.

On the one hand, those who favour the interception of private digital messages and calls say that only by doing so can criminal messages be tracked and the culprits detained. Indeed, there are many examples of violent and sexual criminals (especially in the USA) who have been caught by these methods. A further argument is that people with nothing to hide should have nothing to fear from being monitored, and that monitoring is an exercise in public safety, rather like CCTV or having police officers watch a large crowd for potential trouble-makers. Such arguments are persuasive and are often used by media supporters of interception and monitoring.

By contrast, though, other people point to the fundamental breach of civil liberties which this policing activity involves. After all, they say, we would not allow the police to search our homes entirely at random, or open our paper correspondence without reason, purely on the chance of finding something incriminating. Another counter-argument is the extremely small number of convictions that actually stem from these methods, compared to the overall population. It appears to be true that the security services are most effective when responding to specific information or observations, rather than 'trawling' the entire population's messages in the hope of detecting tiny numbers of criminals.

Overall, I feel that the monitoring of the general population in this way is unjustified, in terms of personal freedoms and the evident lack of effectiveness of such methods. We should urge our police to focus on gaining information through informants and leads from concerned citizens, which would have a higher benefit in terms of conviction rates and consequent public safety.

(317 words)

<u>Examiner's notes</u>

This essay would definitely receive a Band 9 for its clear structure and the way that the writer reports the opposing views before reaching a conclusion.

The intro gives some brief background, and confirms that this will be a 'Discussion' essay. The first main body paragraph reports on the 'supporters' of monitoring effectively by using impersonal or third person structures: 'those who favour' 'A further argument is that.'

The 'opponents' paragraph uses similar structures well: 'By contrast, though, other people point to' 'After all, they say' 'Another counter-argument is'

‘It appears to be true that.’ These phrases give the essay a very objective and academic tone, which is made even stronger by the well-chosen topic-specific vocabulary such as:

to detain the culprits
potential trouble-makers
fundamental breach of civil liberties
convictions/conviction rates
informants and leads

It is not essential for a strong IELTS Task 2 essay to have this level of topic-specific language, but it certainly helps to raise the essay above many others and to justify a Band 9 score. The conclusion feels logical because it summarises and paraphrases the preceding ‘opponents’ paragraph which the reader has just read.

Module 14

Example Task

'A country's museums should always be free for people to visit, whatever the visitor's age, income or nationality.'

To what level do you agree with this idea? Should museums always be free for all visitors?

Explanation of the Task

This is an Opinion > Personal viewpoint type Task. Remember the importance of having a balanced conclusion (an opinion with 'as long as . . . or 'provided that . . .' or similar) after the small concession paragraph. The instructions are inviting you to think about the matter of 'always free' and 'all visitors.' Note how this candidate covers this aspect in his conclusion.

Student's Plan

Essay Type: Opinion>Personal viewpoint

Introduction: Museums' importance; free entry is unnecessary

Main Body:
1 Most visitors able to pay (eg London)
2 Fees can be used to help museums (new displays etc)
3 Many museums are private anyway, subsidies would be impossible

Concession: Free museums are a national symbol; but fees would help them, though not for children etc

Conclusion: Charges are justifiable, provided there are exemptions

Band 9 Model Essay

Museums are a vital part of any nation's cultural life, and high visitor numbers are a desirable indicator of their health and popularity. However, it seems to me that making museums universally free is unnecessary, and even counter-productive, in our efforts to make them more attractive.

For one thing, we should remember that many potential visitors to museums are able to pay an admission charge and would not object to this. For example, in London we see many thousands of wealthy tourists who have paid large sums to travel, and for whom a modest entry charge would be no inconvenience. Indeed, applying a small fee would enable museums to collect revenue which could be used to conserve the exhibits, extend the collections and put on further displays and so on. This would in turn make the institution more attractive, so that more visitors arrive. The Guggenheim museums in the USA and Europe are an interesting example of museums which constantly refresh their contents in this way. Finally, we should remember that not all museums are publicly owned, and indeed there are numerous smaller, private institutions (for example in Russia or the Middle East) which rely on entry fees to survive. Abolishing such fees would be vastly expensive in terms of state subsidies, and would surely have little impact on visitor numbers.

Admittedly, I agree with those who say that universally free museums are a symbol of an equal and advanced society, showcasing national heritage and learning for everyone. However, the use of affordable entry fees (certainly with exemptions for children, the unemployed, students and others) may well add to the museums' effectiveness as such showcases.

Overall, I feel that modest charges are justifiable, and indeed useful, in our efforts to broaden access and improve our museums, provided that nobody is excluded on the grounds of cost.

(304 words)

<u>Examiner's notes</u>

This candidate has evidently planned his essay carefully, because he has quite a complex opinion (*fees are justifiable, and even helpful, but with exemptions*) which he expresses with a persuasive series of ideas.

The only real weakness in this essay for me is the quality of the examples (London, Guggenheim, Russia, Middle East) which don't add much concrete evidence; on the other hand, this can be a difficult topic to think of evidence/examples, and so I would not reduce the Band score because of this. In fact, I would award a Band 9 because of the clear structure and well-developed argument.

The introduction gives the opinion effectively, and alerts me to the 'universally free' part of the argument.

The main body is extremely well staged, with signposting to show the development:

'For one thing . . . For example . . . Indeed . . . This would in turn . . . Finally . . .'

The use of 'Admittedly . . . However' in the concession is a classic way to organise this important section.

The writer uses 'we' ('we should remember etc') to avoid personalisation; where he uses 'I' ('I agree, I feel') this is part of giving opinion in the concession and conclusion, and so seems natural in this context. The conclusion has a balanced view which comes logically out of the main body and the concession, with the point about 'exemptions.'

Module 15

Example Task

It is sometimes said that governments should dedicate a fixed proportion of their country's income to foreign aid each year, and this fixed proportion should always be donated to other countries. Opponents of this idea, however, say that aid should have no fixed proportion, and help should only be sent to other countries at times when it is really needed.

What are the arguments on both sides of this debate? What is your own view on the matter?

Explanation of the Task

This is an Opinion > Discussion type Task. It is not asking you to discuss foreign aid by itself, but the way it should be given (*fixed amounts* or *as necessary*.)

Student's Plan

Essay type: Opinion>Discussion

Intro: International cooperation is important; clarify 'discussion' type structure

For quotas:
1 Moral duty, especially ex-empire countries (UK etc)
2 easier for recipient countries to budget

Against quotas:
1 Budget becomes inefficient, corrupt (eg developing countries)
2 More money would be available for emergencies (floods etc)

Conclusion: Better not to have quotas; better to send funds as needed

Band 9 Model Essay

The issue of foreign aid goes to the heart of how nations should cooperate together, and whether this should be on a 'quota' system or more 'as needed.' In this often heated debate, the opposing arguments can perhaps be summarised as follows.

Proponents of the quota system claim that wealthier nations have a moral duty to sacrifice some of their income to help poorer countries, and that this duty does not rise or fall depending on circumstances. This argument is often used to justify the quota arrangement for former imperial states such as Holland, France or Britain. Moreover, the arguments goes, the fixed proportion system allows the receiving countries to plan and budget reliably, building the foreign aid into their economic calculations.

However, opponents of the fixed donation system respond that this budgetary aspect is in fact the most damaging aspect of the idea. They point out that, if aid money is provided regardless of whether it is actually needed, the funds become part of the recipient country's administrative system, with all the dangers of inefficiency and corruption that this involves. It must be said that fixed aid to some developing countries falls into this trap, as even the local charities themselves will agree. What is more, if aid funds could be held back until times of emergency, such as floods, famine or civil war, the money available would then be far higher and thus would help more people in distress.

To conclude, it appears to me that opponents of the quota system have the more robust argument, with their concerns over unnecessary donations which reduce emergency funding in future. We all recognise a moral duty to help those in need, but surely these resources should be targeted more strictly towards sufferers, rather than sent permanently to government departments to become part of the local economy.

(305 words)

Examiner's notes

The language in this essay shows a good command of both general argumentative terms and topic-specific vocabulary. The introduction provides background to the debate and then outlines the content ('opposing arguments . . . as follows.')

The main body uses noun persons effectively to introduce the contrasting view ('proponents/opponents') and uses third person reporting to avoid confusing these views with the writer's views:

'This argument is often used to'
'Moreover, the arguments goes'
'They point out that'

In the conclusion paragraph, the candidate refers back to this impersonal approach:

'opponents of the quota system have the more robust argument'

This is a useful way to unify the conclusion and the preceding paragraph in a 'Discussion' type essay. General English phrases such as 'goes to the heart of' 'with all the dangers of' 'It must be said that' also help to build a cohesive academic-style argument without using especially formal language.

The topic-specific vocabulary is quite impressive here, with eg 'former imperial states' 'a moral duty to sacrifice some of their income' 'inefficiency and corruption' 'floods, famine or civil war' and 'targeted more strictly' all giving a sense that the writer has read about the topic somewhere in the media.

I would want to recognise this very cohesive structure and effective language with a Band 9 score.

Conclusion to Our Complete Course

You have now completed our course of five books designed to prepare you for IELTS Task 2 writing in both the Academic and the General Training tests. You have seen an overview of the different types of Task 2 questions, and seen many examples of how to make an essay plan for each different type. We have shown you a total of seventy-five Task 2 essays written to Band 9 standard, each one with an explanation of why it is so successful. You have also covered the key grammar concepts to maximize your score, and covered the specialized vocabulary topics which appear in the IELTS test. Finally, you have seen how to create effective plans for your essay during the exam, to put all of this learning into action.

It is important now to practice writing Task 2 essays, using the methods we have explained, before you take the IELTS test. By timing yourself and creating the note plan and the complete essay inside forty minutes, you should be able to develop the skills of analyzing the task, planning, writing and checking your essay to get as close to Band 9 as you possibly can.

Remember that many thousands of people have already used our methods to substantially increase their IELTS score, in many cases after several disappointing previous attempts. We feel that following our advice as closely as you can is the best route to your eventual success in IELTS Task 2.

We wish you the very best for the exam, and for your future plans in life.

Jessica Alperne & Peter Swires
Cambridge IELTS Consultants
cambridgeielts@outlook.com

***

Printed in Great Britain
by Amazon

35310804R00143